COLLECTED I

COLLECTED ESSAYS

Texts on the work of Ana Maria Pacheco

Selected texts : 1983 - 2004

PRATT CONTEMPORARY ART

PRATT CONTEMPORARY ART © 2004
The Gallery, Ightham, Sevenoaks, Kent
England TN15 9HH
Telephone 00 44 (0)1732-882326
pca@prattcontemporaryart.co.uk

ISBN 0 9518049 8 7

Acknowledgements

Our thanks to the authors for the texts and to John Gledson for the translations (full acknowledgements on pages 119-121); thanks also to the photographers: José Israel Abrantes, Maria de Lourdes Pacheco Cordeiro, Richard Denyer, Gill Doel, Colin M. Harvey, Kate Pratt, Kirk Laws, Kelvin Rogers, John Slater and John Whapham; and to Robert Bush and Robert Vas Dias for their assistance.

We are grateful to Salander-O'Reilly Galleries, New York, for permission to reprint the essays by Kathleen Adler: 'Ana Maria Pacheco: Dark Night of the Soul' and Paul Hills: 'Land of No Return'.

Edited and compiled by
Susan Pratt

Picture Credits

Cover, pp 28-39:	*Dark Night of the Soul,* photo © The National Gallery, London
p. 25:	Giambologna (Jean de Boulogne, 1529-1608): *Rape of the Sabine Women,* Loggia dei Lanzi, Florence. © 1990, Photo Scala, Florence.
p. 25:	Terracotta group of "knucklebone" players © The British Museum, London.
p. 81:	Antônio Francisco Lisboa ('Aleijadinho'), *The Last Supper.* Photo © José Israel Abrantes.

Front cover:	*Dark Night of the Soul,* 1999 (detail) photo: © The National Gallery, London
Back cover:	*Land of No Return,* 2002, (detail), photo: Colin M. Harvey
Inside front:	*The Longest Journey,* 1994, (detail), photo: Gill Doel
Inside back:	*Memória Roubada,* 2001, (detail), photo: John Slater.

Production co-ordinated by Footprint Innovations Limited: info@fpiltd.com
Repro by Zone Graphics: zonegraphics@the-repro-house.com
Printed by Principal Colour Limited: info@principalcolour.co.uk

Paper from G F Smith, the paper specialists: www.gfsmith.com
Cover: PhoeniXmotion Xantur 250gsm. Text: PhoeniXmotion Xantur 150gsm

Contents

for David Harper

Foreword

We believe that the making of art is a partnership and our aim is to create the conditions in which art can be made.

We are now in the twenty-sixth year of our unique working partnership with Ana Maria Pacheco, first meeting in 1978 to discuss the idea of printing and publishing a series of etchings. The prints were made and the journey began.

From the outset our aim has been to make our catalogues more than a fleeting record of a temporary exhibition, and we recognise the importance of recording an artist's work through informed texts. We have compiled this book as a tribute to the work of Ana Maria Pacheco and to the authors of texts that we have been fortunate to publish over the years; it includes a number of essays now out of print together with texts published for the first time.

During the last twenty-six years we have had the opportunity to work with some remarkable people and we would like to take this opportunity to thank them all – the authors who have written about Ana Maria, and the museums, galleries, collectors and countless others – for supporting our endeavours.

Bernard and Susan Pratt, 2004

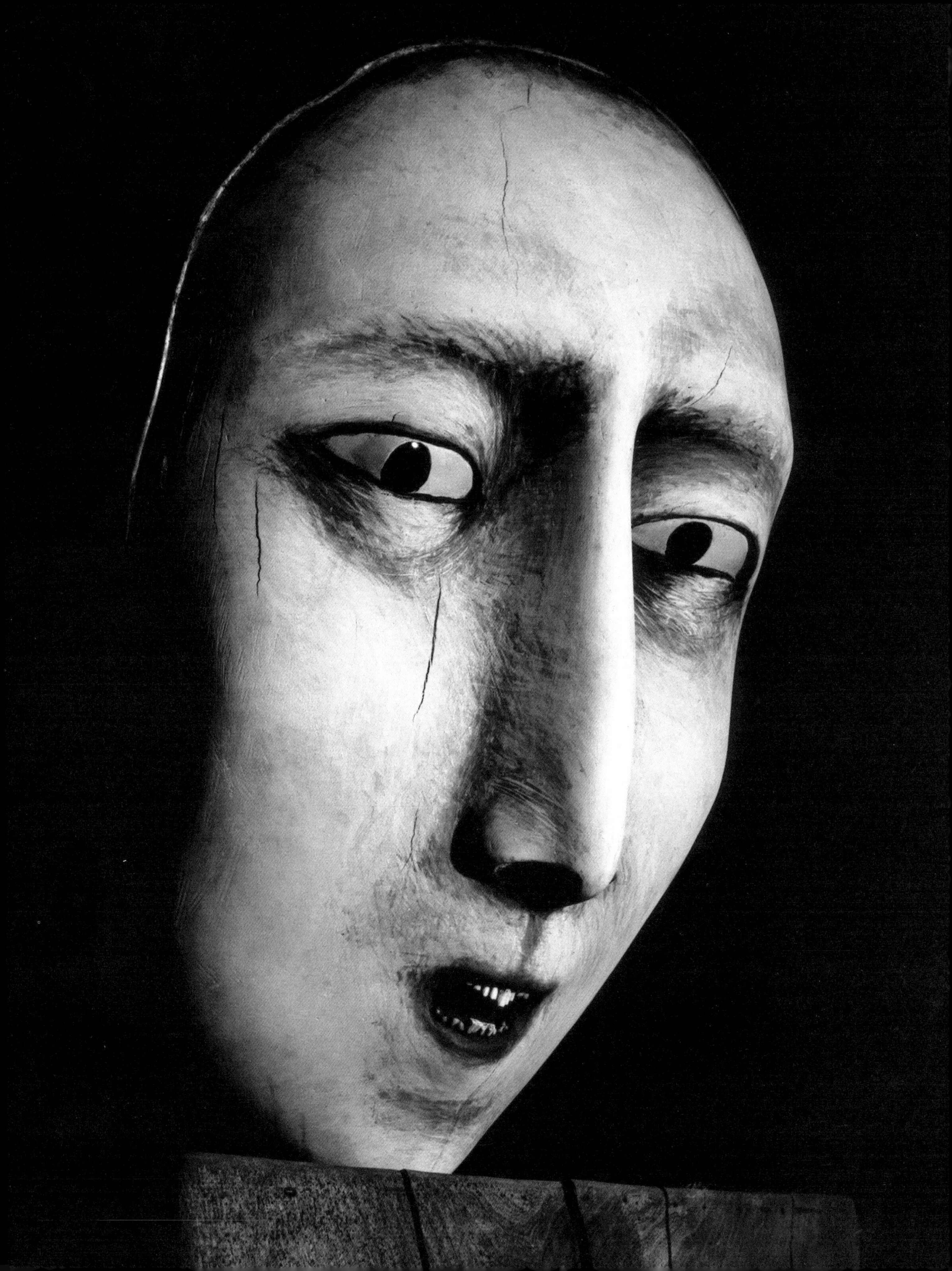

Introduction

John McEwen

When Ana Maria Pacheco graduated her father suggested a woman's role was to be a wife. This was not her intention. "I'm not going to get married", she declared. "What are you talking about! Who's going to look after you?" he asked, flummoxed. "Myself! Thank you very much", she said. And so it has proved – her emergence as an international artist is testimony to that first declaration of independence, as hard won as her formidable output of hewn wooden sculptures. "I'm trying to create bridges", she says: between past and present, high art and popular art, formalism and figuration, her childhood and adult self, colonial Brazil and the European motherland, Catholic and Protestant.

As one might expect her art is unsettling; the physical impact, obdurate individuality, ambiguity and often sinister suggestion ensure division. Her heredity is of its nature divided. Her parents were both Brazilian but her father was from the provincial interior, her mother's family from sophisticated Rio. Their backgrounds were Catholic and Protestant, although neither went to church, and both had experienced calamities. Her father had suffered from the loss of the family fortune in the inter-war stock-market crash; her mother's father, a Baptist minister, had horrifyingly disappeared.

In Britain, her adopted country, Pacheco has found this religious division writ large, her artifice considered a threat. "Ted Hughes puts it very well, the way Puritanism in England expelled artifice", she says. It is true. Emotional embarrassment, spiritual suspicion, still have a tenacious hold. Consider the crude and uneasy obsession with sex shown by tabloid newspapers, TV sit coms and stand-up comedians. It is only now, four hundred years later, that the British seem sufficiently godless to begin to acknowledge and explore the ravages of the sixteenth and seventeenth-century Protestant iconoclasm at the root of this national repression. When political revolution came in France it was the institutions that were destroyed; in Britain it was the art – and the puritan permafrost remains deep. Nonetheless she is one of the few contemporary artists to have had an exhibition in the British National Gallery, and what is more it was a box office hit. Perhaps the permafrost has penetrated those who think before they feel, because it is in an art context that I have heard the 'theatricality' and 'foreign-ness' of her work used as criticisms.

Pacheco concedes there is irony in her art but not the fashionably exclusive and defensive post-modernist kind. It is ironic, for example, that in England she is sometimes dismissed as 'Brazilian', when her very nationality declares her European origin. Brazil is a Portuguese creation. By returning to Europe, she has in her words 'completed the puzzle' of her heredity. Moreover the thirty years she has now lived and worked in England represents half her life and most of her career. Exile has lent detachment. She can analyse her colonialism more objectively from here.

Brazil represents a mixed population of native Amerindian nomads, Portuguese colonists and their African slaves. Pacheco was born and bred in Goiânia, capital of the inland province of Goiás. It was Brazil's coastal strip which evolved in tune with the wider world. Until the last forty years perceptions in the hinterland remained largely true to the early settlement. The original colonists' belief in a mythical world was something they shared with the African and Amerindian populations they ruled. In distant Goiás the sophisticated rationalisations of the Counter-Reformation barely intruded. This was the milieu of Pacheco's childhood.

◂ *Study of Head (John the Baptist II)*, 1990

What excited her most were the great religious processions, especially the candle-lit re-enactment of the Via Sacra on Maundy Thursday. The young Ana Maria took part herself, the proud bearer of huge angel wings in real feathers. "A child doesn't have 'beliefs', it has an overwhelming sense of reality. At university I changed intellectually but that childhood experience tints your perception of the world forever."

The climax to this mourning came on Good Friday, when everyone gathered in the church and in utter silence the sculpture of the dead Christ was exposed in a coffin. "It was this enormous catharsis. Many people would be crying. For one moment everybody was part of one thing", she recalls. It is a lesson she has never forgotten – the way a single artefact bound the community, concentrating feeling and negating social distinction. "The most crucial thing about sculpture is physical presence", she says. It is this physical presence she finds particularly lacking in contemporary sculpture, the word 'sculpture' itself rendered meaningless by its blanket application.

Her childhood was less regulated than similar childhoods are today, when anxious parents tend to 'fill all the gaps'. She was left to her own devices. Study was liberation, discipline grounded in piano practice imposed by her profoundly musical mother. "I was brought up a free spirit. I wasn't forced to go to church. I went because I loved it. But to play an instrument you have to be forced, and my mother was strict in that. I would never have had the discipline to make the sculpture I do if I hadn't had to learn the piano." Music remains central to her life. A great attraction of London for her is its world-class programme of concerts and recitals.

Her formal education was Catholic. "It was quite wonderful. It was based on traditional French education, so, very humanistic. I studied Latin for many years and – nobody would dream this now – *everybody* had to learn music in secondary school!" As a teenager she nonetheless became aware of the Catholic/Protestant divide: the one feminine, forgiving, permissive to the point of apathy; the other rigid, full of rectitude but ultimately stifling.

There was much reading, a thorough grounding in Greek thought and mythology. It was a classical Western education of great refinement existing in a society of pagan-empowered Catholicism, swept away in the 1960s by the adoption of American pragmatism, something she deplores. As she notes, "Greek thinking and Greek myths are still very close to us".

Pacheco attended the state and Jesuit universities in Goiás simultaneously. At the Federal University she studied music; with the Jesuits she took the fine art course. Fine art included a thorough art-school training, but she completed a post-graduate scholarship in Rio in music. She denies she was brilliant, just obsessive. As a post-graduate she practiced the piano ten hours a day but eventually admitted her personality was not that of a performer. "You have to crave applause. I was never like that. I don't need 'success' in public terms, I want to succeed in what I propose to do and by doing what I want I feel fulfilled. I think it's hard in life to do what you want. And I love solitude."

Her instinct was to carve and this has also remained one of her preferred pictorial methods. She is a master of intaglio and the woodcut, and even her technique as a painter is as sculptural as she can make it – her surfaces stiffened by gesso so she can work them vigorously and often incisively. Working pictorially is also a release. "The way I sculpt is very slow and can be restrictive. Printmaking and painting help me resolve things in sculpture." They are revitalising.

Vitality is surely the secret of the magnetic force of her work. Her large wooden tableaux are not naturalistic and yet their power is as palpable as life. They hold the visitor in suspense. When she describes the work of the great Brazilian sculptor

Antônio Francisco Lisboa ('Aleijadinho') (1730 or 1738-1814) as "stripping sculpture to a bare kind of human experience" and being "primitive but at the same time very sophisticated", she could be describing her own work, although she demurred when I suggested it.

Aleijadinho was a half-cast, a personification of Brazil, that cultural mix which, as the world of football knows, can prove an unmatchable combination of power and grace. Pacheco's cultural divisions are different but no less potent. Her work has indeed created bridges, as the crowds at her exhibitions, the devotion of her collectors and the eloquence and international range of the twenty-three essays in this book testify – those by John Clark, José Lobo, Brendan Prendeville, Nicolau Sevcenko, Annela Twitchin and Colin Wiggins ('Reclaiming the Baroque: a drama in wood') published for the first time. Yet she still feels she belongs 'neither here nor there'.

This is memorably expressed in her most recent sculpture at the time of publication, *Shadow of the Wanderer*, 2004: a life-size study for one of what is intended to be a group of twenty larger figures, showing a muscular young man carrying an old man on his back. It is a traditional image – recalling the legend of Aeneas carrying his father Anchises from the burning ruins of Troy – but could hardly be a more pertinent metaphor for the rootlessness which, in its various ways, is now the global norm. "There is the idea of 'the wandering Jew', who is maybe the prototype of the refugee, but all of us carry our past." And bringing attention to the inseparable shade thrown by the piece, she adds: "None of us can escape its shadow". She regards the figure as a son carrying a father – another increasingly familiar contemporary burden, as more and more of us survive into a helpless old age. But as always with Pacheco the truth is in the making. "I'm not a designer. I like to work without knowing what's going to happen. The figures evolve and suddenly they're there – or not!" She laughs; a citizen of the world, her art a rare and powerful expression of what is now the prevailing human condition.

In the Region of Shadows

Brendan Prendeville

The key to Ana Maria Pacheco's work lies of course in her sculpture, and the essence of her sculpture is that it is the opposite of effigy. Unlike a waxwork, which may fool us for an instant before it becomes uncannily lifeless under our gaze, her figures (and not only the sculpted ones) grow inwardly in our imagination over time, acquiring life. To mention effigies at all, however, is to acknowledge that there is some ground here for comparison: the study for *Shadow of the Wanderer* is typical of Pacheco's sculpture in being fleshed and clothed with colour, and in bearing facsimile eyes, embedded teeth. Yet here both practice and effect are wholly different from what would apply with the inanimate waxen double of a film star or a politician; we could not possibly mistake the eyes of her anonymous and strangely-proportioned beings for those of actual persons, but they genuinely carry, for us, the sense of seeing, as no waxwork ever can.

It is a notable fact that in contemporary art the effigy (cast, moulded, modelled, preserved, 'plasticated') has become virtually an obligatory mode for representing human beings (and animals) in three dimensions. Most contemporary figure sculpture is closer to the waxwork than it is to the religious or myth-inspired sculpture of former times, other cultures. In the first case, we may see an uncanny reflection of ourselves, lacking only life; in the second, a thing other to ourselves, reflecting back to us a different aliveness. Ana Maria Pacheco's sculptures are contemporary precisely in addressing this modern difficulty in imagining life, which in turn arises from a difficulty (much dwelt on by a very different contemporary artist) in imagining death. Imagining death is what she ventures here, both in the series of oil pastels and in the sculptural study of a younger man bearing an older one, which several drawings rehearse.

Study for Land of No Return, 2000

Pacheco has looked to past art for help in her present quest. We can catch echoes of Böcklin in the screen of funereal pines in the largest *Hades* oil pastel; Goya and Rodin in the choric crowd in one of the *Wanderer* drawings; Renaissance and Baroque precedents, for the intertwining of bodies in the sculptural group and studies. And the polychrome sculpture of her native Brazil has been often invoked as a general source of inspiration. Yet it would be a mistake to see her work as a summation of these precedents, for it operates strictly in terms that belong to the present.

Her technique, for example, is quite untraditional, though in its own terms highly exacting. It is by luring us with the fascination of the worked-upon that the sculptures invite us to come close. Pacheco carves and abrades the wood into body-like contours, which she then gives a flesh of variegated hue. This she does by blending an emulsion on the surface, working rapidly with (of all implements) cotton buds. She has visited every square centimetre in order that we, in turn, may pay close attention and, in giving our time, impart duration and life to what we see. What we do see, looking closely and standing back again, is a figure (or figures) whose being is concentrated in a single gesture of the whole body, and given its intensest focus in the face. Notice how often in her work she pulls heads down onto or even a bit below the shoulders, closely binding together the expressive and active regions of the body.

Study for *Shadow of the Wanderer*, 2004

This manifestly holds for two of the three figures enclosed by darkness in the largest of the *Hades* oil pastels *(Hades I)*, though the third is a stark exception to the rule. In the Orpheus-like being who turns to unveil a shimmering Eurydice we may catch Pacheco's imagination at work. In him, as often, she gives a powerful rendering of nakedness. It is erotic, and his entire posture – not only the gaze – is caught up in

Hades I, 1998

an act of looking that is between desire and apprehension. The whole of his life is in that look, it is a life-and-death look. On either side of it are two faces that, in contrast, are isolated visually by clothing that surrounds them. The head of Eurydice, risen on a long neck, veiled, and cut off from her still more remote body, has narrowed and unseeing eyes, lost to the gaze that seeks them and lost to life.

The drawings and the sculptural study for *Shadow of the Wanderer* show the artist searching for a gesture, a posture, of an intensity equal to the Orpheus. We may feel that this Aeneas and Anchises group speaks to us topically of asylum-seekers. If so, it is only by first giving, once more, a bodily life to vision. In one of the two large drawings, the weight of the younger man's burden is emphasised, his head hanging, eyes closed; in the other, he looks around furtively or in fear, while the elder's head sinks into blind shadow. Venturing from his land and burdened by his origin, the wanderer must tread carefully, learn a new alertness.

All their life is in their gaze: this is a condition Pacheco's figures aspire to, and would evoke in us.

Hades III, 2004 ▾

New and Recent Prints

Annela Twitchin

'But ask now the beasts and they shall teach thee: and the birds of the air and they shall tell thee...'

Job 12:7

A Modern Bestiary, text and images, has a very long ancestry. In the ancient world, animals and especially birds were studied with some respect because they were believed to reveal by their behaviour the will of the Gods. The first bestiary, the Physiologus, was written in Greek and most probably in Alexandria during the fourth century. It consisted of a series of descriptions of animals both real and imaginary derived from various ancient sources: Indian, Hebrew and Egyptian animal lore and from the writings of classical philosophers such as Aristotle and Pliny.

With Latin translations it became widely distributed throughout Europe and eventually was translated into many languages. The Physiologus was most popular during the Middle Ages, a popularity which can be partly explained by the Medieval belief that all God's creation, including animals, was intended to provide examples to humanity of the correct way to live. Hence the Physiologus became the core text for the development of the bestiary in England during the twelfth century.

Since then the tradition of the bestiary, text and image, has continued to have unabated appeal as evidenced by the many versions and variations created through the centuries. Among the most pleasurable are the bestiaries created by Lewis Carroll, Apollinaire, James Thurber and, most recently, *A Modern Bestiary* with poems by George Szirtes and screenprints by Ana Maria Pacheco. With wit and invention in word and image, many of the animals and birds, the traditional exempla of the bestiary, are given very contemporary connotations, be they political, ecological or social.

In *Rottweiler*, the Hannibal Lector visage menacingly masks the uncontrollable violence of the impotent being depicted, whose only power is purportedly over a dog with a reputation for violence. Reminder also of a certain recent royal powerlessness resulting in the loss of one canine to another! 'By their dogs ye shall know them.'

Hare by way of contrast alludes to a literary and folkloric past. Szirtes' allusion to William Cowper, the eighteenth-century poet whose intense love for nature and animals, especially the three hares (their companionship enabled the suffering poet to share with them a paradise garden on earth), is exquisitely imaged by Pacheco. Her vernal paradise returns us also to the one she created for Solomon and Sheba in the painting completed whilst artist in residence at the National Gallery. But the arrow piercing the hare's breast touches on something beyond the cruel sport of men so detested by Cowper. The arrow signifies death not just in physical but in emotional terms. For there is a belief that the hare is the spirit of a broken-hearted maiden who appears as a white hare to haunt the man who pierced her heart till such time as he meets his own end.

Many of the screenprints accompanying the poems include a box, long a part of Pacheco's pictorial vocabulary. *Crocodile, Giraffe, Mandrill, Platypus, Rat* all have its mysterious presence, the container, the concealer of what? We all carry our box of cultural baggage with us along with the memorabilia of our existence. Pandora's box of woes, of course, we also carry. *Rat* and his box are suspended in a balance – a scale of justice.

Crocodile, 2004

Eagle, 2004

Interestingly, the maligned rat is increasingly replacing the dog to sort out the man-made environmental problem of landmines – he is lighter in weight and learns much faster than the dog!

The power of the eagle, magnificent bird of prey, is traditionally seen to be of a noble nature. *Eagle*, poem and screenprint, suggest power of another order: political. The severed head recurrent in Pacheco's visual imagery is here a grim reminder of the ruthless violent reality of so much political policy. But birds, even longer than animals, have been enlisted to solve environmental problems. Today in China it is the eagle that is being bred to help the authorities rid the country of a plague of giant gerbils who are reducing the country's grassland to desert.

From magnificence in size to brilliance in miniature the hoopoe has a history, mythical and factual, that is fascinating. Its ability to detect changes in the atmosphere that herald electrical storms and earthquakes has been observed and respected since ancient times. The role of the hoopoe in the meeting of Solomon and Sheba was so beautifully depicted in Pacheco's National Gallery work in the 1990s.

A Modern Bestiary, through word and image, takes us beyond the pleasures of response to the traditional exempla of the bestiary. There is a shift towards the serious need to respect the role of animals in the world we share together. We are reminded also of the need to renew awareness of their mythic and folkloric relationship to man, if we are to retain our humanity in the fullest sense.

Fables like the bestiary have a long history extending back beyond the popularisation of them by Aesop. Probably primitive peoples whose lives were in much closer contact with the animal world told tales of their encounters and engagements with each other. Fables long used as moral instruction remind us that once the world was conceived of as a unity; folklore continues to remind us of the magical powers of animals and we continue to respond to both myth and fable because we regret the loss of this world and contact. The first fable in this set of ten drypoints, *Fables 1,* depicts the monkey astride the dolphin. The dolphin in ancient times, and still today, is treated as a friend of man. It was told that in the past many a shipwrecked sailor was carried to shore on the back of a dolphin. Here the fortunate creature is a monkey. Having carried him to the safety of the port of Piraeus, the dolphin asks if he is an Athenian and whether he is familiar with Piraeus. The monkey answers in the affirmative to both questions but assumes Piraeus is a person rather than a place, thereby returning the life-saving courtesy with untruth. Enraged by this deception the dolphin dives into the depths of the sea, drowning the dishonest and self-deluding monkey. His very human expression of a less than engaging kind gives emphasis to the nature of man as exploiter.

Fables 1, 2001.

The ferocity depicted in *Fables 2* again functions with both a past and present significance. Aesop's fable uses the belief that hyenas change their sex each year so that last year's male is this year's female. Humankind has the understanding that we are constituted of both male and female principles. This combination has done nothing to resolve the sexual squabbles of the hyenas – the battle of the sexes never ends!

Emulation through envy captures the camel *(Fables 3)* in an ungainly attempt to dance, due to his supercilious self-delusions that he possesses the same agility as the dancing monkey he scorns.

The contrast between the shimmering silver sleekness of the fox and the creaking craquelure of the crocodile *(Fables 4)* visually conveys something of the dialogue between these two: boastful upturned snout of crocodile – quivering keenness of intensely self-aware sharp-snouted fox!

Fables 3, 2001.

How easy it is to allow one's own misfortune to be wallowed in out of all proportion to its reality is revealed by the admonishing frogs *(Fables 5)* who ask the ass what kind of moaning he would make if instead of his temporary setback he was permanently relegated to life in a bog!

The regal eagle *(Fables 6)* teaches the ponderous tortoise a lesson. So great was the creature's desire to fly that he persuaded the magnificent bird to elevate him to a great height from which once dropped he promptly learned the error of his wingless way!

Fables 7, 2001

The wily wolf *(Fables 7)* persuades a heron with the promise of reward to remove a bone from his throat. Reward? He promptly rounds on the bird for not taking satisfaction in still being alive to tell his tale!

There are many tales in Aesop concerning the cat but Aesop was not the only person to invent cat proverbs. There are hundreds of them in as many languages. They can be divided into two categories, no pun intended – cautionary and character. Our cat and cock *(Fables 8)* re-engaged in a verbal battle of self-justification – the cat for eating the cock and the cock for the necessity of his staying alive. Governmental self-justifications spring to mind!

Fables 10, 2001

The final fables in this series also have contemporary relevance. The snake and house ferret's ferocious squabbling *(Fables 9)* draw out the innocently interested mouse who is instantly turned on by the belligerent pair. As state politics show, people who interfere in quarrels can become victims of both sides.

The gentle stag seeing an enraged lion *(Fables 10)* gives warning of what might follow, seeing as how the beast was always intolerable when relatively calm: a sober reflection on hot-headed men and the harm they can do when in power.

Of the several hundred of Aesop's Fables, the ones chosen by Pacheco for her series clearly have relevance to the situation today – politically, domestically and ecologically. Her drypoints, with an exquisite precision in the depiction of her animal protagonists, extend the traditional range of animal-human analyses in art. Like Grandville before her and unlike so many others who have illustrated Aesop, Pacheco does not anthropomorphise. Rather it is our human posturing that is mirrored in the mimicry of our often absurd body language by her accurately delineated animal protagonists.

Griffin, 2000

Much of classical mythology was an attempt by Greek and Roman cultures to interpret the remains of creatures that no longer existed in their worlds. Explanations were made of fossils that incorporated earlier oral legends and stories told by nomadic peoples. Several of the creatures in the series of drypoints entitled *Beasts* originated in this way, for example the Griffin.

Scythian nomads of the seventh century BC told to Greek travellers the tale of the land to the East where gold deposits were guarded by fierce lion-like creatures with hooked eagle-like beaks. A variant on this tale was that the beasts were fighting to protect their nesting grounds. Gradually the Griffin motif began to appear in classical art and architecture, but the archetype was none other than the protoceratys fossil found in the Hindu Kush where the beak, wings, nests and deposits of gold would have been seen by any traveller. How many other mythical beasts, one wonders, have their legendary origins in fossil remains.

Chimera, 2000

Several of the fantastical beasts depicted by Pacheco 'evolved' over centuries into composite creatures of terrifying aspect. One such creature is the Chimera that found its way into mythic retelling in Homer and Hesiod. Both described it as a creature with the body of a lion, the tail of a serpent and the head of a goat springing out of its back. The origin of such a creature may have derived from the winged lion, many images of which existed in Mesopotamia from the third millennium BC. Blurring of

Burak, 2000

Quetzalcoatl, 2000

Domestic Scenes 1, 2000

Domestic Scenes 3, 2000

the image could have transformed it into a goat's head. When cosmic beliefs changed from a goddess-ruled system to a male-dominated one, the winged lion became an evil monster. The Chimera became a deformed image of the mother goddess and of all the evil that men can think of women! Cultural systems and beliefs are still being overturned – by male domination. Pacheco's *Chimera* is a reminder of this.

The Koran records that Mohammed was the third and final prophet of the true faith of God, following Moses and Jesus Christ. Legend relates that Mohammed was carried from Mecca to Jerusalem on his milk-white steed Burak, who is sometimes described as having a human face, the body of a horse with wings and the tail of a peacock. Pacheco's beautiful *Burak* flies above ideological conflicts.

Although Quetzalcoatl is an Aztec name, he is a god of such importance that he played a role in the pantheon of virtually all the other Mesoamerican deities. He is the god of sustenance, self-sacrifice and rebirth. However, he originated as a water god. In the first myth in which he appears he is called "precious serpent" and was the spirit of the waters. Sometime later the idea of a snake representing both the terrestrial and the celestial comes about and *Quetzalcoatl* emerges as here depicted.

Two of the Brazilian beasts represented are the Boitatá and the Inhatatá. Some versions of the Boitatá legend say that it is a huge fire serpent which lives in the river and attacks other animals to absorb their energy and light to keep its fire in the water. Pacheco represents the version that says it is a bull-like creature which spits fire from its mouth, but in reality it is said to be the soul of a wicked person. The Inhatatá is a bird of southern Brazil that runs through the pampas bringing fear to all who see and flee it.

The Brazilian Yara, like the Russian Rusalka and the Sirens of the classical world, were creatures of beguiling beauty who lured men to their death in water. Sometimes these water spirits were thought to be the spirits of unmarried women. In the Ukraine there was a ritual known as Rusalka when it was believed that the water spirits came into the fields and birch groves, bringing water and fertility to the land.

Herein lies the fascination and importance of Pacheco's series of *Beasts*, be it of the Basilisk, the marine version of the Centaur, the Unicorn or the beasts already referred to here. They remind us of the overlapping cycles – cosmic, agricultural, human life and death cycles – and that these co-exist in imaginative ways with the acquired scientific knowledge of our universe. They are the reminders of the mystery that still stirs our senses and fulfils our need to feel as beings on the boundaries of the unknown.

Deceptively entitled *Domestic Scenes*, suggestive of soothing domesticity and conjugal bliss, the ten prints pertaining to stories from Boccaccio's *Decameron* and Chaucer's *Canterbury Tales* are something quite other. We have in the Boccaccio prints the testing of love – husband of wife, the neurosis of possessive love be it father for daughter or brothers for a sister – and we have the revenges exacted which rebound as they should do on the perpetrators.

The violence voiced in these stories has a resonance with that of our own time. Powerless to retain the affections of the female heart, many of Boccaccio's male protagonists resort to the removal of the heart of a rival and serve it up as the sweet dish of revenge. One of Pacheco's plates *(Domestic Scenes 7)* captures the cruel moment of pleasure as the husband reveals what his unsuspecting wife has been enjoying in his seemingly simple sharing of a meal. This horrific communion with her lover has reverberations in the recent macabre case of Armin Meiwes who advertised for a person willing to allow his body to be dispatched, dismembered and eaten. This strange sublimated union of bodies took place. What residue of ritual had remained in the minds of these two men from times that long preceded the ritual of revenge with which culturally we are still so much at home?

The obsessive need to test the totality of an obedient and acquiescent love is the subject for *Domestic Scenes 1.* In this image the cruelty of Gueltieri's actions, his endless testing of Grizelda's love, is reflected in the cruelty of his face. The contrast with the passive, submissive modesty of Grizelda is striking and it lends strength to her self-imposed submission. The frenzied violence depicted in *Domestic Scenes 8* leads to submission of another order. Boccaccio's ironically titled Nastagio and Beloved Girl tells what is in store for the Beloved if she does not yield to him. The young lady of the story will after all marry her persistent suitor to avoid an end as the one enacted before her. But, he still does not control her heart! *Domestic Scenes 3* depicts a Boccaccio story we are all familiar with and fascinated by – witness the many richly coloured canvases devoted to its disturbing theme. Lizabetta was so loved by her brothers that they disposed of her lover, decapitated him and buried his remains. Her grief at his absence drew his spirit to her to reveal the deed and place of internment. The head is soon reburied in a pot of basil and tended daily by Lizabetta's tears. Discovery and further removal of the object of Lizabetta's devotion leads to her own demise. Once again death unites and the living are left with loss.

Domestic Scenes 4, 2000

Domestic Scenes 10, 2000

The Chaucer tales are more misogynous and bawdy: cuckoldry, cupidity and concupiscence are their themes. Not so much the passions of the heart or aristocratic honour as the lewd lust of elderly bodies for younger ones who in turn, if married to old men, seek only to cuckold them with younger lovers. Some of the tales chosen reflect sins decried by the Church. The Pardoner's Tale *(Domestic Scenes 9)* relates how the outcome of greed is almost inevitably death. In the Reeve's Tale *(Domestic Scenes 10)* the greed of the crooked miller leads to a beating for him and the loss of both his wife's and daughter's honour.

Lust is the theme of both the Miller's and the Merchant's Tales. *Domestic Scenes 4* depicts the garden of delights – that is for the seemingly innocent child bride of the elderly blind man (blind in more than just the physical sense) whose hand she holds. In the foliage of the tree we see the fruit of her desire! The Wife of Bath's tale *(Domestic Scenes 5)*, told by the feisty partner of five husbands, an expert in the matrimonial game, reverses the sexes' roles in the desirability stakes. A seeming old crone can lust after a handsome-bodied youth, the twist in her tale being that women have wiles and guile beyond the comprehension of men who believe in money as the only currency with purchasing power in relationships. Chaucer's *Canterbury Tales* find resonance in the mores of society today, as Pacheco has shown in her choice of the stories and tales to be conveyed in the succinct subtleties of her visual language. Through superb technical and imaginative skill the drypoints *Fables* and *Beasts*, so small in size, still convey a sense of our engagement with the animals, actual or mythical, as taking place in an infinite expanse. With *Domestic Scenes*, larger in size, we are confined to the experience of the protagonists, claustrophobically closed in by the world of their own cruel dysfunctional emotions.

Bandits I (Lampião), 2001

Bandits II (Tiradentes), 2001

The set of four etchings entitled *Bandits* represent real historical figures. Lampião, the leader of a notorious gang of bandits during the 1920s and 1930s, was captured in 1938. Both he and his gang were decapitated and then toured the country at the government's expense! The tradition in portraiture is to study the human face in its individual physiognomy to convey something of the sitter to the spectator. The shock of lack of eye-to-eye contact in these severed heads leads us to search for the seat of the soul – where is it? The violence done to the human form is deeply unsettling. Through subtle etching technique the delicate shading in each print creates a

Hairy Legs of the Queen of Sheba 1, 2001

Hairy Legs of the Queen of Sheba 4, 2001

Sheba and Solomon in the Garden of Earthly Delights, 1999, (detail)

Sheba and Solomon (i), 2004

surrounding no man's land between our life and the bandit death. The richness of the technique that shapes and shades each head seems to set them within the sky and soil of Brazil. The dark intensity of death is assuaged by passages of light that merge into a timeless cerrado landscape.

Since the nineteenth century the allure of the 'historical' Queen of Sheba has given rise to many imaginative realisations of her in literature, in opera and in painting. On the silver screen her celluloid image has been immortalised by Gina Lollobrigida strutting her stuff in a series of diaphanous gowns straight from a Paris fashion house of haute couture! There is as yet no finale to her fascination, as an exhibition held in the British Museum in 2002 and dedicated to her personage evidences.

In 1996, when Ana Maria Pacheco was appointed Associate Artist at the National Gallery, one of the works resulting from her tenure was the painting with predella entitled *Sheba and Solomon in the Garden of Earthly Delights.* Sheba appears as a dusky oriental in Arabic shift that does not clothe an hourglass figure of the Western ideal. The promise of seductive delights that she embodies is slyly suggested by the setting, by the sheer tactile and eye-ravishing beauty of the garden's flora and fauna. In solitary prominence in this rich verdure sits the hoopoe, the tiny bird instrumental in the making of this meeting. It was the hoopoe who flew the world to find if any place existed which was not subject to Solomon. Finally he came to a rich, lush land ruled by a beautiful woman who had never heard the name of Solomon nor of his greatness. Soon the hoopoe became the go-between, the carrier of the letter that led to the actual meeting of the two rulers. But also depicted in these panels are scenes that relate to Sheba's sovereignty of state in her own lands, so that disposing of an unwanted husband by decapitation presents no problems!

Pacheco has further explored the relationship between Sheba and Solomon in a series of prints entitled *Hairy Legs of the Queen of Sheba.* Prior to the arrival of the beautiful Sheba at his court, Solomon was led to believe that she was not quite the woman that her reputation for great beauty led one to believe. It was rumoured that she had hairy legs and the hooves of a donkey in place of delicate little feet. Hence the first image – Sheba with a donkey mask, and Solomon wondering: does her beauty mask a donkey? Is she making an ass of me? Male cunning prevailed over female guile and a court of glass was constructed under which water and fish gave the impress of a pond. Naturally Sheba raised her skirts in an attempted crossing and so revealed her legs, truly hirsute. Travesty about the feet though. Solomon insisted on depilation and Sheba's submission became the first instance of subjugation to the ideal of feminine beauty imposed by men.

The artist's book, the livre d'artiste, has, and especially in France, a unique place in the art of the preceding and present twenty-first century. The creation *Sheba and Solomon* (artist's book) makes a magnificent contribution to this genre. Working in collaboration with Ruth Fainlight, who had been inspired to write a sequence of poems after seeing *Sheba and Solomon in the Garden of Earthly Delights* at the National Gallery, both poems and prints give the ancient story's source a decidedly twentieth century twist. The small format of this volume, encased in crimson leather, contains in its pages a mytho-religious world clothed in the imaginative colour of its verbal and visual language.

The vignettes, like the marginalia of medieval bestiaries and illuminated books, and like those uniquely developed by Blake in his illuminated books, are here given in their exquisite embroidery of flora and fauna the most recent continuation of this tradition.

The first image, *Sheba and Solomon (i),* like the National Gallery painting, places our protagonists in the perfumed verdure of a paradise garden where man and beast co-exist harmoniously. Or do they? The lion, whose carved image adorned the fountain in the National Gallery painting, is placed here between the royal personages in its own living regality. Perhaps all is not as it appears in the paradise garden. Only the hoopoe, instrumental in the meeting between Sheba and Solomon, knows. He is the bird who sees, whose power to foresee perhaps extends beyond the phenomenal world.

Sheba and Solomon (ii), 2004

Solomon, reputedly the wisest man who ever lived, was ruler not only over men but over beasts, birds, demons and spirits and, of course, he could commune with all in their various tongues. Solomon and hoopoe, *Sheba and Solomon (ii),* convey this rich concatenation of sounds.

Sheba had posed three riddles to test the wisdom of Solomon, which proved greater than the conundrums set by her. By way of return, Solomon exacts a promise which, if broken, will give him the right to satisfy his desire for her. To promise to take nothing of Solomon's seemed simple enough to fulfil. But there is many a slip between cup and lip! Slaking her thirst brings us to Sheba and Solomon in bed, *Sheba and Solomon (v).*

Sheba and Solomon (iv), 2004

Sheba and Solomon had significance for many cultures: Christian, Muslim and Jewish traditions all make reference to this powerful pair and the meeting that took place between them. The relationship between Sheba and Solomon takes many different turns in the telling, but most versions of their encounter have her return to her own realm after mutual enrichment of engagement.

Fact or fantasy? Even today, in the twenty-first century, we respond to that which eludes the realm of reality. So – to Sheba in a boat, an image that is elusively satisfying for us all, *Sheba and Solomon (iv).*

We are all familiar with the painting by Goya known as *The Burial of the Sardine* depicting the end of carnival time and the beginning of the forty days of Lent – the symbolic burial of merriment and pleasure during the days of fasting and prayer. There are of course other allusions in Goya's painting, to the power of Church and State, but primarily it is the representation of a ritual that heralds a period of reflection and meditation on the great mystery of faith.

The series of eight drypoints entitled *Misfortunes of a Sardine,* image by miniature image, also serves symbolically to represent a meditation, not on the mystery of faith but on the journey made during the course of individual and creative development. The humble sardine has become both guide on the journey and the pictorial personification of the creative process itself. Part of this process involves a referral to, and renewal of, visual vocabulary created in former works. The journey begins with a reference to an earlier *Terra Ignota* as the sardine parachutes down onto an unknown shore. There are allusions also to the Bosch-like figures suspended in the air in one of the *Luz Eterna* panels. Sardine's parachute, like Daedalus' wings fashioned by him to escape enclosure in the labyrinth of his own creation, becomes the means by which, upwards or downwards, creative exploration continues. The pathway is rarely clear. The Sardine encounters a giant and, as one recalls, the Golden Age and the Bronze Age were followed by the Iron Age when giants were confrontationally cruel, lustful and destructive. Sardine versus Barbarian, but Sardine aka artist has, like Circe, the power to effect some, though as we see, not total transformation of the brutish being.

Sardine Arrives, 2003

Sardine fights back, 2003

To descend into the underworld, the realm of the dead, to commune with the shades of the deceased, was an experience granted to few living beings. But first the golden bough had to be brought to Cumean Sibyl in her cavern at the entrance to the

Sardine enters the underworld, 2004

Sardine sails away, 2004

dark realm. Aeneas gave the golden branch to the Sibyl and she became his guide in the journey to find his father, Anchises' shade.

Here we see the Sibyl give the golden bough to the Sardine and she journeys alone. The river Styx with its ferryman, Charon, the Tartarean river of hell and its guardian Cerberus are passed by, and eventually the Sardine arrives at the Land of Joy, home of the blessed. Here she is reunited with her friends, with the creatures that appeared in *A Modern Bestiary*, in *Fables* and inhabited *Sheba and Solomon in the Garden of Earthly Delights*. A re-encounter with past achievements. Aeneas journeyed to the past to be informed of his future – the founding of Rome – which he then returned to the present to fulfil. *Misfortunes of a Sardine* ends its sequence with an image of a boat in which Sardine simply sails away – into an unknown future? As we know the boat has universal significance as a cultural symbol – the ship of fools, the ship of death and in its passage through water, the start of life. It is made a metaphor for life's achievements, both personal and creative.

The trajectory of Pacheco's creativity has always developed in response to such cultural symbols, but her cultural awareness and creative responses are not defined or dictated by one cultural world view alone, as her work demonstrates. There is also the recognition that below the rich diversity of cultural traditions there is a residue of the collective unconscious, the remains of an underlying universality of consciousness below the millennia of change.

In his short story, *The Third Bank of the River*,[1] the Brazilian writer João Guimarães Rosa touches on the human psyche, on the root of a human being's existence. The narrator of the tale is a small child, son of the man who is about to leave his family on land to spend the rest of his days sailing the river '. . . so deep and silent and wide that you couldn't properly make out the other bank'. With the passage of time the son, now father to the man, wished to exchange places with the ancient rower, his father, who was agreeable to the change but fear led to abandonment of the exchange. "I know now that I will end my life in the shallows of this world, but at the point of death want to be taken and laid in an insignificant boat – I – river."

Neither the life force nor the creative process function or strive to journey endlessly from one bank to the other. It is the 'third bank' that is metaphorically the aspirational goal, the pursuit of both the life force and the creative process. So now we know the direction in which Sardine set sail.

Land of no Return, a recent important sculpture, is crucial to our understanding these marvellous prints that have brought Pacheco into an intimate relationship with authors both long dead and living to reveal her own creative originality. The prints, like the sculpture, relate to past works and presage future ones. There is no land of no return. The passage between past, present and future is embodied in the journey made through personal, private, intellectual and creative experience. We always travel in return, we are connected with the former travellers in our lives, whatever forms they take. Transformation is ever eternal renewal – the embodiment of the creative process. Ana Maria Pacheco's printmaking is her way of renewing and redefining the artistic self, for which we as her spectators are profoundly grateful.

Notes

1 João Guimarães Rosa: 'The Third Bank of the River', in *The Jaguar and Other Stories*; translated by David Treece, pp157 and 164; published by Boulevard Books, 2001.

Land of No Return

Paul Hills

Ana Maria Pacheco's *Land of No Return* consists of seven figures in a darkened setting. Coming to know this work initially involves physical movement, circling round, looking from far and near, which in turn prompts a journey in the imagination. From the intended point of approach, we first encounter the isolated figure of a woman, tall and youthful in a spectral white dress. Whereas the other figures are carved from trunks of lime, she alone is carved from cedar-wood, and the veins of the wood show through the whiteness of her dress to suggest the quickening pulse of spirit shining through body. With lips parted and head turned, she is animated, seemingly apprehensive, as if she has just awakened in a new world. One notices that she wears silver sandals and that – in a virtuoso feat of carving – her heel is raised. She appears to float. Perhaps she is a soul suspended between two worlds, a Persephone, or a even a goddess, kin to the Aphrodite 'with her silver sandals' seen in a vision by Odysseus. Her gaze is directed towards three women absorbed in a game or ritual of cowrie shells. They hold the gilded shells in their hands, and more shells lie gleaming where they have been cast on the ground between them.

These three fates or three sisters, in contrast to the ethereal soul in white, are dressed in indigo blue; rather than rising into air, they crouch with bare feet pale upon the dark ground. Another contrast is less obvious but suggestive: their ears are entirely hidden whereas the ears of the standing woman are fully revealed – as spirit all her senses are alert. One of the players looks up at the apparition in white and so invites us to peer into the darkness beyond her, there to discover three naked men in violent argument. Even from this distant view it is obvious that the men are taunting each other but their shouts and stifled cries cannot be heard by the sisters with the cowrie-shells. Carefully controlled lighting contributes to the sense of a gulf between the soul in white and the trios, male and female, on either side.

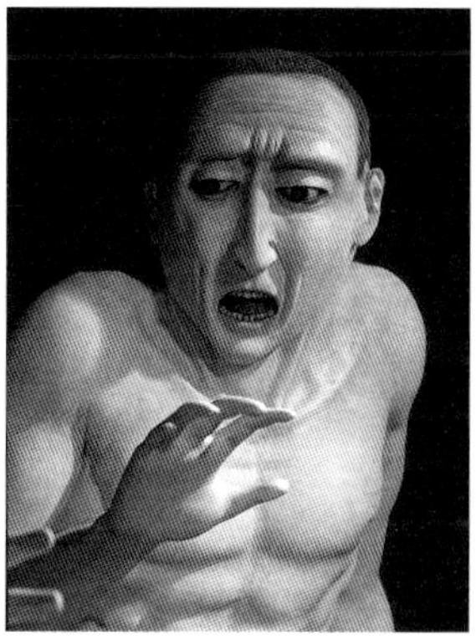

Land of No Return, 2002, detail

For anyone familiar with the Western convention of the male nude, as dominant from the Renaissance to the nineteenth century, these fighting men are deeply disturbing: to fathom the power of Pacheco's art we must confront our disquiet and ponder its origin. From the start we are uneasily aware that the violent trio recalls the nude warriors celebrated in the tradition that runs from classical Greek sculpture and vase-painting, through Pollaiuolo's fifteenth-century print of fighting men, to Michelangelo's models for multi-figure groups, such as the *Victory* or *Samson and the Philistines*, to the scenes of male combat by Rubens and David. Pacheco has never before carved figures in such energetic movement, or paid such attention to musculature: the result is a virtuoso performance. Yet something is disturbingly different from the traditional rhetoric of the nude warrior. Slender-waisted, her fighters anxiously draw breath; and all of them appear more scared than heroic, their over-large heads grotesquely distorted by primal emotions of fear and rage. Unlike their classical counterparts, Pacheco's men are not clothed in the propriety of a graceful pose: they are naked rather than nude; violent individuals rather than ideal types; and – most shockingly – men whose exposed sex is at the centre of their violence and their anxiety. Not surprisingly, visitors to the studio who saw *Land of No Return* in progress shied away from confronting this nakedness, turning in relief towards the women.

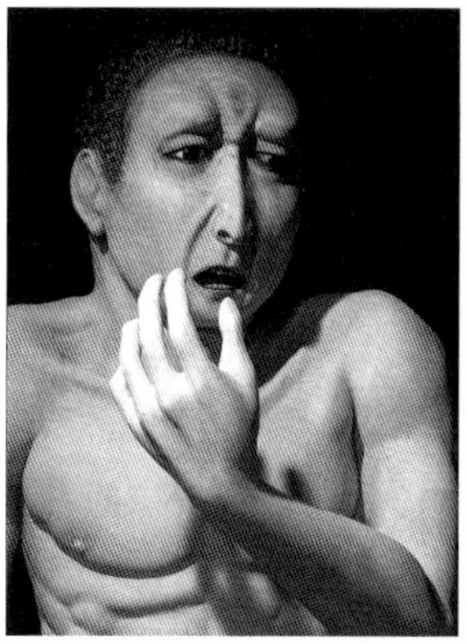

Land of No Return, 2002, detail

During her time as Head of Fine Art at Norwich School of Art, Pacheco attempted to reform the practice of the life-class because she believed the conventions of the life-

room had increasingly divorced bodies from life-stories and so crippled the capacity of students to develop a figurative imagination. In *Land of No Return* it is clear that Pacheco has absorbed a tradition and through a remarkable exercise of technical skill – rather than any facile mockery – challenged it on its own terms. Allusion to sources is part of the strategy, and she readily points to Giambologna's *Rape of the Sabine Women*,[1] a photograph of which is pinned to the studio wall. At first Pacheco intended that her struggling men should be interlocked in a single block like Giambologna's marble, but soon realised that it would be almost impossible to transport. As always, the solution to physical problems, coupled with the work of carving, shaped the narrative and its form. The crouching Roman at the base of Giambologna's spiralling group became detached as a taunted victim.

Giambologna
(Jean de Boulogne, 1529-1608)
Rape of the Sabine Women (1)

How does allusion to Giambologna enlarge our understanding of *Land of No Return*? Working in the late sixteenth century, Giambologna's elegant nudes appealed to the Medicean Grand Dukes of Tuscany, and they commissioned his compositions of warriors overcoming enemies or carrying off women as trophies, and set them up in public places as emblems of victory and symbols of princely dominance. Like the noble bodies of the heroes, subjects were almost interchangeable: as Giambologna remarked in a letter, "The aforesaid figures can be interpreted as the rape of Helen, or even as that of Persephone, or as the rape of one of the Sabine women." All are celebrations of power and in this respect herald the Baroque, the style favoured by the absolutist monarchies of the seventeenth century; and hence the artistic language imposed upon Brazil by its Portuguese Catholic conquerors.

Ana Maria Pacheco was born and first trained as an artist in Brazil, before settling in Britain in 1973. In conversation she has remarked on how the Portuguese attempt to stamp out pagan superstitions in Brazil was never entirely successful; instead Catholicism and other beliefs and rituals, some of Indian, many of African origin, survived in symbiosis. The establishment of the Inquisition in Brazil ushered in 'a time of fear' among the people which survived, Pacheco felt, into her childhood in the city of Goiânia. In this light, her subversion of the image of the victorious male nude responds both to artistic and political colonisation. From a position of profound understanding, it turns the rhetoric of power against itself.

'Knucklebone' players (2)

Like the men, the trio of women in *Land of No Return* have sources in the art of the distant past. The most striking is a terracotta, probably made in Taranto in southern Italy in about 330 BC, of two girls playing a game with knuckle-bones.[2] In contrast to Giambologna's monumental marble, it is small in scale, domestic in subject, gentle in spirit. Dating from pagan antiquity, centuries before both the Imperial Roman and the Christian era, this terracotta has been associated by Pacheco with a ritual practised in Brazil which originated in pre-Christian Africa. In Brazil it is known as Buzios and performed by a teller with sixteen cowrie shells, which are cast and interpreted according to the configuration they make upon the ground. Cowries, of course, are widely regarded as emblematic of the female sex. In Africa and elsewhere they were often treated as currency, indeed one species is named *Cypraea moneta*. Gold was the great treasure of Brazil, plundered – or raped – by Europeans, an unending catalyst of strife and brutality. For Pacheco the aphorism of Saramago, "Brazil is fertile with cruelty and diamonds", is apt. So in her recasting of Buzios, it is less the telling the future than commenting on social morality that is to the fore. In *Land of No Return* the cowries are enlarged and gilded to become nuggets of shining gold and, instead of a single teller, Pacheco has formed a ring of three, who – like the Rhinemaidens of the *Nibelungenlied* – guard their treasure. Telling a fortune and guarding it have been elided.

Buzios, 1997

◂ *Land of No Return*, 2002, detail

In conversation Ana Maria Pacheco speaks of how narrative provides the thread, how the story determines the forms, yet how the story is liable to take a new turn as the figures take shape. Early on she discovered that, like the girls with the knuckle-bones, her tellers had to be crouching low, close to the ground, with bare feet finely articulated. She realised that she would have to make them more realistic than anything she had made before. Then in the process of carving the great limewood trunks as they lay on their backs, each of these three sisters emerged as different in age and each characterised by distinctive rhythms running through the folds of drapery, the curls of hair or bands of head-dress. The manner in which these rhythms guide our reading of the story – leading attention to the suspense in the hands, to the poise of the head and the intent of the gaze – is wonderfully assured. The folds are credible as costume yet they transcend mere externals to shape an encircling visual music which eddies and flows in a mysterious pattern of binding and loosening.

But the story does not end with the carving. The painting takes almost as long as it is painstakingly built up over a green ground for the flesh. In the faces particularly, the colouring is not simply naturalistic pigmentation but modelling – modelling which interacts with the three-dimensional carving, modifying it and inflecting its expressive range. What is more, the painting endows the figures with their own luminosity and their own darkness, which in turn becomes visually meshed and confounded with the light and shade of the installation. Experiencing *Land of No Return* is a bit like passing a threshold into another world – or 'other-world' – and finding oneself walking around inside a painting.

▾ *Land of No Return*, detail

The most haunting of the sisters, with her hair bound in a white head-dress, is indeed a painting come to life. She is a reincarnation of the fortune-teller by Georges de la Tour.[3] Both have the same inward gaze, the same aura of sadness in which foreseeing is eclipsed by foreboding. Commenting on the affinity, Pacheco suggested that in seventeenth-century Europe, as in Catholic Brazil, the woman as seer had been deprived by church and state of her oracular role, outcast as a trickster, even a witch – like the three sisters in *Macbeth* – yet enduring on the margins poignantly aware of loss. Something of this impotence hangs over the three fates. In the space between them they wait for the oracle to speak, for the goddess to come down. Like all the inhabitants of *Land of No Return* they are suspended in a purgatorial limbo. Yet they are not ghosts: they are as real as the many generations of mothers in Márquez's *One Hundred Years of Solitude* who watch and foresuffer all.

In an interview in 1998 Julia Kristeva criticised contemporary installation art for losing faith with the visible and went on to argue, "We need to learn anew how to negotiate both the visible and the invisible, and this has to start with paying a tribute to the visible." *Land of No Return* pays such a tribute while simultaneously alluding to the problematic role of representations. Like all great literature and myth, Pacheco's realism invites us on a journey in which we may begin to learn again how powerfully the visible is grounded in the invisible.

Notes

1 Giambologna (Jean de Boulogne, 1529-1608): *Rape of the Sabine Women*, Loggia dei Lanzi, Florence. © 1990, Photo Scala, Florence.

2 Terracotta group of 'knucklebone' players, Hellenistic Greek, about 330-300 BC © The British Museum, London.

3 Georges de la Tour, *The Fortune Teller*, ca. 1632-35, The Metropolitan Museum of Art, New York.

Memória Roubada, 2001

. . .The cabinet opens its doors onto the effects of violence; more than a simple theft, there has been an armed robbery, murder, or genocide in the name of someone or something – a form of mockery or contempt. Outside, there to be contemplated, lies the heart pierced by those beautiful, noble daggers, their blades gleaming.

To bring this crime to light, the work gives us its core – it only examines its heart. Through what's left behind, everything else can be intuited. The spectator at one moment identifies with the heads in the cabinet, but at the next feels the pull of pure suffering. It's impossible to get closer, for the space is protected by a mysterious glass jar, surrounded by a halo. Therefore, we have to be careful: modesty joins hands with charity, and creates this instant, made for withdrawal and meditation. . .

José Lobo, text extract, 2001.

Ana Maria Pacheco's 'Memória Roubada': a Latin American Work

José Lobo

After its discovery, Brazil stayed as it had been, where the white men had found it. As if the giant had no desire to leave the beaches, he turned his back on the continent, staring out to sea in the hope of sighting the ships that would take him back to Europe. As time passed, these illusions gradually faded, Brazil took heart and decided to explore its own interior, giving the impression that it was launching itself on a supreme adventure: the search for its own soul. It moved away from the seacoast, rediscovered old routes that led down from the coastal ranges into the interior, navigated down the rivers, penetrated the virgin forests, and entered the unknown land without measuring distances, heedless of dangers, led on by the need to reveal whatever was hidden just ahead, or a little further off.

This version of history, however, will never be accepted by anyone with any sense. Even in those days of acceptance of extraordinary events and blind faith in miracles, other more realistic observations referred to the hunt for Indians as the real imperative that led men to delve into the jungle. Before they left, they attended religious ceremonies, for the intention of converting the heathen to Catholicism – that is, of bringing them into the fold of Holy Mother Church – was regarded as praiseworthy. The Indians would certainly be baptised. They would take on new names, and would exchange the words learnt from their parents for others, from a more universal language inherited from Latin. They would cover their bodies with some kind of cloth, and would become familiar with shame. However, before they began their new life, as a prerequisite for the consumption of the goods and services of the white man's international market, it was necessary to enslave them. This seemed the most sensible solution, since it was the most economical. Indians, then, could well be the motivation for these 'bandeiras' [lit. flags], the name given to these enterprises. Preying on Indians became the high-risk sport of the eighteenth century, with perils, adventures and lots of adrenaline. The mercantilism of the time approved of the idea of mixing the useful and the agreeable; and the greater the profit, the more agreeable it was. Seizing Indians became a successful activity because another, more profitable activity was linked to it. Fortunately, the news arrived in São Paulo of something perhaps more valuable than the naked bodies of indigenous girls: gold. In the outback reached by the 'bandeiras', little nuggets of gold innocently decorated the river-banks. They were devoured with the eyes, followed by grasping hands; then they were placed in the memory – there was gold here. Diamonds, too, flashed in the riverbeds. Somewhere, there must be emeralds, why not? Nothing would be wasted, not even in the imagination: even dreams would be written down in the form of heroic chronicles. But cruelty could not be recounted in the raw; on the contrary, it had to be covered with the ornament necessary to obtain the approval of their good readers: it had to be done in the appropriate fashion, the way the nobility knew how to decorate their stories.

Such niceties on one side, the basic truth of the matter was a product-change in the contemporary market. Fortune's wheel gave a turn, and a new cycle came, keeping foreign interest in the distant colony alive. Before, there had been Brazil-wood, but the intrinsic value of the stones and precious metals guaranteed a level of profitability never before attained. The economic cycle is fickle, like love; both are like a flame, and both die down. The first steps taken by the discoverers, cutting down the jungle, had already produced some articles of value. The Brazil-wood taken to

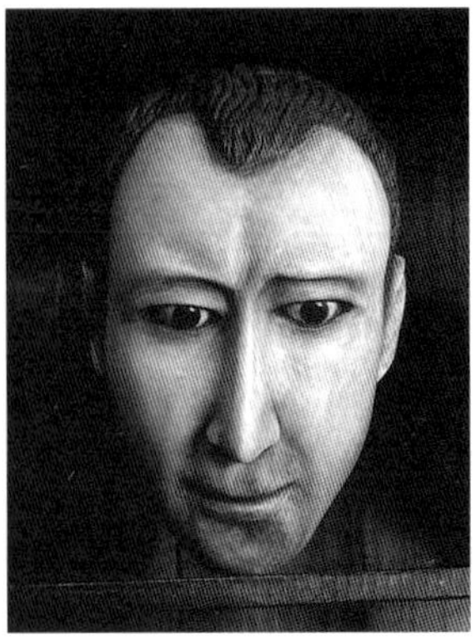

Memória Roubada, 2001, detail

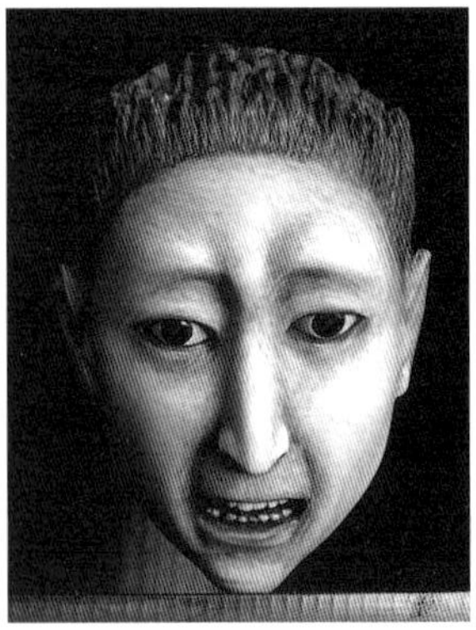

Memória Roubada, 2001, detail

Memória Roubada, 2001, detail

Europe permitted men to dye their clothes the colour of blood, the symbol of royalty and the privilege of the powerful. However, purple, in all its splendour, would not be complete if its adornments were missing: jewels to give it a greater dignity, gems to shine in a cardinal's ring.

Adventures, dreams, dangers – business too, and politics, for the crowned heads of Europe took care to fill their coffers. They zealously guarded their colonies, and by force of law and the right issuing from the cannon's mouth, they administered their lands beyond the sea, and gave heathens the possibility of eternal salvation. In Europe, the kings and ambassadors, princes and cardinals reached agreements with each other; in South America the 'bandeiras', as they made their way into the continent in search of its treasures, had already stumbled on the Central Plateau. The interior, landlocked part of Brazil was discovered. The time had come to put a stop to the adventure, and, under the strict vigilance of the Captains-General, to organise trade and social customs according to the designs of Providence, identified with the will of the king. In the end, civilisation would reach the interior of Brazil, where there was nothing more beyond the thick jungle. Tax-collectors made their presence felt at the ends of the earth, extracting from one and all what they owed the Crown. Everything had to be legally established, so as not to leave gaps where informal activity could take place, even if it was the search for a person's soul. Alongside the temporal power, the Church was also present, and outside the Church there was no salvation.

The eighteenth-century gold cycle is one among many movements of colonial exploitation that make Brazil into a transient phenomenon, something that can't go beyond the medium term, an ideology in permanent expectation of what might happen in the future, if some day the chains of underdevelopment are broken; this hope removes its right to existence in the here and now, and of having its true soul uncovered.

The eighteenth century will go down in history as a time of intense economic and political activity. In colonial Brazil, it had cultural effects whose resonance can still be felt in our own day. One has the sensation that the saga begun at that time is asking to be continued, as if Tiradentes's horrific death had not been the end of a search for freedom and justice.[1]

Memória Roubada ('Stolen Memory') by Ana Maria Pacheco, is a work profoundly committed to the cultural heritage of the eighteenth-century 'Golden Age'.[2] This commitment is more than a choice, and is better understood as a destiny for someone born in Goiânia, and thus linked to the inheritance coming from Minas Gerais, where the history of landlocked Brazil begins; it is a history that reaches into Goiás and spreads out into the regions of Mato Grosso, even more remote. These three states, Minas, Goiás, and Mato Grosso, had their roots in the Catholicism of the Counter-Reformation and the gold of colonial Brazil. From this amalgam of faith and power, adventure and wealth, of an urban life surrounded by a powerful structure of independent rural establishments, one might expect a creative synthesis to be born, based on authentic local manifestations. There might have evolved an original cultural expression, had Portuguese repression not acted against it with such violence, and imposed silence. The Inconfidência was suppressed, and centuries of silence followed; but at the beginning of the third Millennium, Ana Maria Pacheco takes the theme up again in *Memória Roubada.* It is impossible to calculate the consequences of her stubbornness, this renewed acceptance of risk. This, at a time when globalisation is driving from the face of the earth the differences and contrasts that make up the individuality of every people and every soul. Ana Maria Pacheco does not make art for the market, and is not worried by the whims of fashion, or by the marginal, promotional aspects of the life of an artist. Even so, interest in her work is growing because of the mystery inherent in every piece she has put in the public domain. It is difficult not to feel the prophetic force of the ancient Sibyl in this challenge, this provocation. With *Memória Roubada*, Ana Maria Pacheco offers us a sign, a clue for victims curious enough to be tempted into the labyrinth; it is a thread to find the way back, and it must not be lost. *Memória Roubada* tells us, amongst other things that have been said about her, that Ana Maria Pacheco has an origin; her career has a starting-point, she was born in Goiânia.

Memória Roubada, 2001, detail

Belo Horizonte, Goiânia and Cuiabá, three capitals in the Brazilian interior, define the axis of our 'landlocked', baroque culture, to which even Brasília, so innovative in many respects, had to pay homage. When Lúcio Costa wrote in his account of his project, whose aim was Brazil's re-encounter with its interior, that he began to develop his plan for Brasília with the sign of the cross, he reaffirmed the influence of Catholicism in these lands. When Oscar Niemeyer reproduced stylised columns in the Palácio da Alvorada (lit. Dawn Palace, the presidential residence), he took up the old design of the large verandas of colonial architecture, those of the plantation houses. It had to be that way, for we cannot deny our origins. For the Latin American soul, the Baroque is a call that comes from those origins, and from which it cannot escape. The landlocked culture of Brazil is marked by this late Baroque, the fruit of the imagination of its creators, mostly people of mixed blood, like its greatest exponent, Antônio Francisco Lisboa (1730 or 1738-1814), O Aleijadinho.[3]

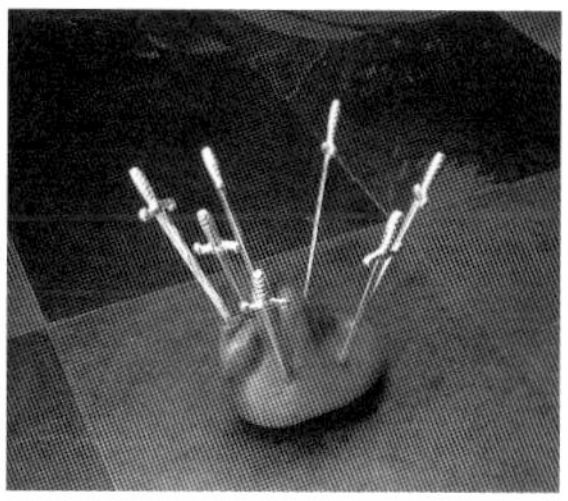

Memória Roubada, 2001, detail

Ana Maria Pacheco's art, because it has this visceral commitment to its own authenticity, becomes an instrument for the investigation of the collective soul of the people she herself belongs to. An imaginary line, the Equator, crosses the earth. Below this line the imagination seems to have more time and space. In this South, people pay no attention when they are ordered to act with urgency. They proceed calmly, with perseverance, letting each day take care of itself, surviving and looking for their stolen memories. The artist, in her turn, is looking also. When making an engraving or a sculpture, when she pares the material down, as if getting rid of irksome appearances, she seems to be looking for a reply to her insistent, earthbound search: 'Where is it?' The moment has not yet come for us to know *what* she will find; we can instinctively feel the direction she is going in, but there is a long journey to be faced in her search for what is there, still further down the road. We are looking at a work of art which is not decorative, though it transcends simple political engagement. From its very origins, Ana Maria Pacheco's work could not avoid this obligation to its destiny; but to this remote cause are added circumstantial elements, in a challenge which she cannot refuse, as an artist of her time and with a profound interest in everything contemporary culture has to offer in the form of a question or an answer. But, if her remote origins have not succeeded in making of Ana Maria Pacheco an artist who might be accused of indulging in archaisms, neither has the latest fashion managed to make her into the flavour of the month. Sculpting or engraving, Ana Maria Pacheco overcomes superficiality and cuts ever more deeply, carving in the direction of something inward; or perhaps her chisel is looking for something beyond that again. The adventure doesn't rest content with mere circumstance, but searches for something more immanent; her material seems to owe her an answer. Michelangelo also hammered out the knee of his Moses, but even if the stone could speak, it would not be enough; Ana Maria Pacheco's development takes her towards the final confrontation, the greatest challenge, towards transcendence.

Memória Roubada, 2001, detail

Ana Maria Pacheco, then, makes art as if she were looking for the substance of the duty imposed on her, of what she has to do. All of us Latin Americans, too, are engaged in the same search. We need to find the memory that has been stolen from us. The portrait so far made of the Third World is still unfinished: this is why we have to bring our memory back to the surface.

Ana Maria Pacheco's *Memória Roubada* is a work which deals with the Latin American drama from a position of advantage, free of the superficial emotion brought on by excessive proximity; rather, collective feelings here receive protection, to be refined and reinforced by knowledge.

We should mention the contribution that Ana Maria Pacheco, an artist with a solid intellectual background, has received from European culture since she moved to England, where her career has been consolidated. This contribution gives us the best example we could wish for of a successful interchange, of a mutual respect that has evolved towards a deeper, more fraternal feeling. Seen this way, the new global world will be desirable if it promotes unity in diversity, without excluding anyone.

We have spoken of *Memória Roubada* from the position of someone who is a character in her plot, part of the real basis from which she started, of the circumstance which demands explanation. These are the only credentials we can offer to justify such audacity. Here we are, in Cuiabá, the capital of Mato Grosso. We are at the geodesic centre of South America, at the remotest point of its interior, related to the country's coastline in the same way the centre of a circle is to its circumference. We live in a depression which goes down towards the Pantanal, and though so distant from the coast, we are only two hundred metres above sea level, at the entrance to the mine, living on top of the remains of the gold that has been taken away. *Memória Roubada* is thus a coloured sketch, the road to heaven, a rainbow to take us to the northern hemisphere, and which can take us still further. This work belongs to all Latin Americans, whose soul, neither genuinely Latin nor exclusively American, was created mestizo so that it could, with the help of a higher synthesis, move in the direction of transcendence; only art can help us fly upwards in this fashion.

Translated by John Gledson

Notes

1 Tiradentes (literally the toothpuller) was the nickname of José Joaquim da Silva Xavier (1746-1792), a relatively humble participant in the Inconfidência Mineira, a movement for independence from Portugal which took place in the interior of Brazil, in the gold-mining area, in 1789, and was repressed by the Portuguese authorities. Tiradentes, who showed considerable courage under torture, was the only participant in the conspiracy to be put to death: he was hung, drawn and quartered on 21 April 1792. He has since become a national hero and 21 April is a national holiday.

2 'Golden Age': this phrase is taken from the classic account of the Brazilian gold-rush in English, C. R. Boxer's *The Golden Age of Brazil, 1695-1750.*

3 O Aleijadinho literally means 'the little cripple'. A mulatto, he was the greatest sculptor and architect of the Brazilian colonial period, doing all his work in the gold-mining area of Minas Gerais. Perhaps his most famous work is the series of statues of the prophets outside the church of Bom Jesus de Matosinhos at Congonhas do Campo. He suffered from a disabling disease (it is still uncertain exactly what) which meant he lost the use of fingers and had to have the chisel strapped to his wrist.

Reclaiming the Baroque: a drama in wood

Colin Wiggins

"Sculpture, at least the way I do it, is very restricted. Apart from anything else, you are dealing with the space that you actually live in. A chair, for example, occupies the same space. That creates an enormous difficulty, for you to break through the visible world to the world one wants to deal with, that is the invisible."

For an artist dealing with 'the invisible', Ana Maria Pacheco makes sculptures that are remarkably solid. Her installation, *Dark Night of the Soul*, began its life as a collection of tree trunks. By September 1999, those tree trunks had become nineteen figures, some over life-size, others smaller. Despite their human characteristics, these figures refuse to deny what they really are: tree trunks. They look hewn, rather than carved. Delicate details, such as faces or hands, do nothing to alleviate the overwhelming sense of heaviness. They make no attempt to disguise their woodenness, to conceal their organic origins. Indeed, they flaunt it.

Walking amongst these sculptures can be an eerie experience. A central character is bound and hooded, naked and transfixed with silver arrows. He is surrounded by a circle of four upright figures, massive log-men, who stand like a menacing Woodhenge. They appear to be enacting a silent ritual of sacrifice and blood-letting. Other figures exist outside the inner circle, talking, gesturing, feeling. Concentrate on looking at one character, and others appear in your peripheral vision. Suddenly one of them moves, not of course a sculpture but another viewer whose stillness has momentarily deceived you. Spectators nervously laugh with one another as the spell is broken. In the half-light of the installation this can be deeply unnerving. Audience participation is an old device in the theatre but unexpected in an art gallery. However, with Pacheco's work it is crucial. The audience shares the space with the artwork and that space is carefully manipulated. Artists such as Caravaggio, Rubens or Guercino, in their great Baroque altarpieces, understood how to manipulate the space, as part of the whole visual experience, by careful control of the light. So does Ana Maria Pacheco. The walls are painted a deep blood red. The room is blacked out, to the extent that some of the characters seem to disappear in the shadows. Spotlights starkly illuminate the only two naked figures. The first is the victim figure, bound to his column. The other is a small boy who gazes at the tormented adult with an expression that seems to waver between curiosity and shock. The surrounding circle of log-men is illuminated principally by light reflected off the body of the victim. They loom in the half-light, solid yet ghostly. A softer light is cast on the other figures, who are arranged in clusters around the central group. They either interact with one another or stare fixedly at the bound victim.

Work in progress, 1998

Ana Maria Pacheco is a consummate craftswoman with obsessive notions about the quality of finish, an artist to whom the acquisition of skills has been an essential part of her history. Wood sculpture is a craft that dates back centuries, with personalities like Riemenschneider and Donatello elevating it to the highest of arts. By the twentieth century however, artists who insisted on demonstrating a high level of technical accomplishment became treated as outsiders. Ignoring fashion, Pacheco demands that we not only notice, but that we are amazed by the skills involved in the production of her work.

Work in progress, 1998

The carving and finishing of the figures is only the start. Colouring the sculptures, both broadly with brushes and delicately with cotton buds, is an even longer process

Dark Night of the Soul, 1999, detail

that includes painting, sanding down between layers and repainting, slowly, painstakingly. The faces of the wooden figure carvings of the Baroque period, to which Pacheco's work alludes, are by comparison often gaudy and crude. The finished surfaces of a Pacheco head have an exquisiteness, like high-quality needlework, that one is tempted to call 'feminine'. Only when she has achieved this degree of hand-made perfection, will the artist allow a work to be called finished.

The pristine surfaces are only part of the story, because they are used solely to represent areas of skin, or occasionally fabrics. Other areas are left coarse and rough, made all the more powerful by contrast. Each process emphasises the other. The highly-finished areas act as a foil to the burnt and blackened gougings that represent the main bulk of many of the figures. A chain-saw is used, a tool that can hardly be used with precision and the exposed wood is then charred with a blow-torch. These resulting rough-hewn areas become seen as overcoats or cloaks, the chain-saw's vicious slashings working in stark opposition to the smooth sheen of the skin areas.

Since the first showing of this work in the National Gallery in the autumn of 1999, cracks and fissures have appeared in many of the figures. These are left deliberately unrepaired by the artist, as if she is allowing the sculptures to complete themselves. The figures add their own finishing touches, using the natural process of drying out and splitting. They crack, to reveal their splintery insides and remind us that they are, after all, just pieces of wood.

Dark Night of the Soul, 1999, detail

Despite her insistence on impeccable technique, Pacheco's sculptures do not set out to trick us into thinking that they are something other than what they are. The finished sculptures are certainly not illusionistic. The heads are vastly out of proportion. Some characters have nails driven into their heads to stand as hair, in the manner of an African tribal fetish, as Pacheco draws on art from widely different traditions in order to forge her own visual language. Other figures have hair represented with the same charred surfaces as the coats of the log-men, having been similarly burnt with a blow-torch. None of this is to do with illusionism. Yet the paradox is that these inert tree-like figures seem alive, they convince us that they feel and they have souls. Part of this is to do with the teeth. Pacheco uses false teeth obtained from a dental supplier. She sets these tiny things into the heads in crooked rows. False teeth are meant to go unnoticed in a living head, but with these sculpted heads they are perhaps the first things we are struck by, even before the extraordinary gazes. Like paintings by Francis Bacon, the mouths become repellently attractive, adding to this quality that makes us think 'they're alive'.

Dark Night of the Soul, 1999, detail

The eyes play an equally important part. Made of simple black discs of polished onyx, they look nothing like human eyes. Their size and colour however, make them seem like black holes that suck in the light. They convince us that these wooden people can actually see, making the idea of the gaze one of the most memorable features of this installation. The giant log-men stare at each other, implying a variety of different emotions. They are psychologically, as well as compositionally, bound to one another. Amongst the smaller figures a mother with her child seems stunned by what she witnesses. A group of arguing figures stands some little way off. The two women in this group look alarmingly conspiratorial, while a brutish and angered young man clenches his fist menacingly. His face, with its flat forehead and curving nose, seems to be South or Central American, with its reference to Aztec sculpture. He is one of the figures whose hair is represented by nails banged into his head. One other figure shares this physiognomy and hair type. She is small, female and crouching. She gazes tenderly at her fellow nail-head, and watches him rage. Nearby is another child of the same size as the little naked boy, this time female and clothed.

Softly lit and dressed in yellow, she has turned away from the central group, although one feels there is little doubt that her wide, wide eyes have seen everything. Also in this group is another boy, slightly older, who crouches and covers his face with a hand. He is able to see but he chooses not to. Finally, isolated from all of the other figures, a tall middle-aged woman stands alone. She stares fixedly, standing in her own gentle pool of light. Her black eyes indicate she is perhaps deep in shock as she gazes, apparently traumatised, at the victim. It is for us to decide what is going on, as we walk amongst the figures, for this work has no definitive story. The image of the arrow-man was initially inspired by the legend of the early Christian St. Sebastian, who was punished for his faith by being shot with arrows. However, Pacheco's title of the piece, *Dark Night of the Soul*, omits his name. Therefore, we are free to see this victim-figure as Sebastian if we want to, but other readings become possible. Traditional representations of the saint show him gazing up to heaven, still alive but suffering. This torment did not actually kill him, for he was rescued and nursed back to health before his eventual martyrdom, a much less visually dramatic clubbing to death. Most usually, it is the arrow torture that has been favoured by artists.

The Dark Night of the Soul, 1993-4

Pacheco's piece, though, is no traditional representation. By adding the hood, she immediately wrenches the old story from the safety of the past and drops it firmly in our own time. The artist is keen to distance herself from what she calls a 'pamphlet kind of art', but the political implications are none the less undeniable. One of her sources for *Dark Night of the Soul* was a photograph, originally published in a Brazilian newspaper, showing a victim of one of the many notorious South American death squads. He is kneeling, virtually naked and bound by his neck to a wooden post. He has been garrotted. Pacheco had a copy of this photograph, which she tore from a magazine, taped to the wall of her studio when she was working on her piece, and the visual similarity is strong. Such images are now so commonplace that we hardly notice them as they flash by on our television screens. When the image is frozen though, as in a news photograph, we can study it at our leisure. Our horror is compounded by the sense that we have become voyeurs at a gruesome spectacle, consumers of a product that has its origin in the suffering of an unknown individual. We are powerless to intervene but we still stop to stare. We are glad that it is him, not us.

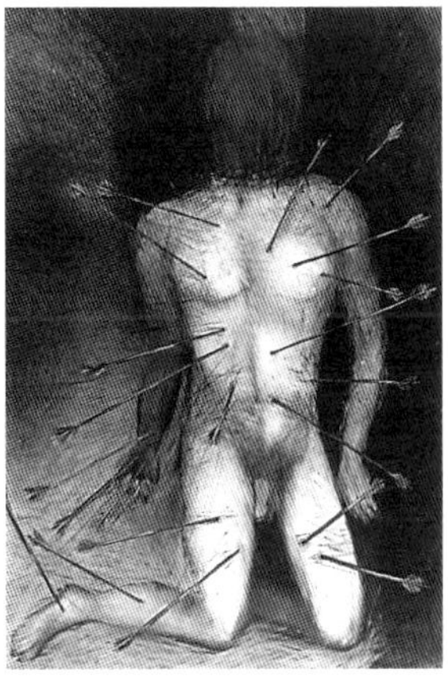

Target 1, 1997

These viewers who walk amongst Pacheco's figures are put in the same position. We are witnessing a barbarity. As we walk amongst the figures, we make eye contact both with other viewers and with the sculptures themselves, staring at the shiny black discs that seem to stare straight back at us. We acknowledge our fellow viewers and likewise we can see ourselves in relation to the uncannily human, yet not human sculptures. There is one exception however. The only figure who is deprived of sight is, of course, the hooded victim. We are separated from him by lack of gaze and are related to the other figures by the possibility of mutual gaze. Slowly the realisation dawns on us, that both we and our fellow viewers have become participants in this cruel drama. As spectators, when we mistake each other for one of the sculptures, it is of course always as a clothed figure, never as the victim. His nakedness and his blindness keep him firmly apart from us. While we are watching this event, whatever it means, we have been placed by the artist on the same side as the tormentors.

Narrative and theatre are central to Pacheco's art. It therefore stands close to the Roman Catholic art of the Baroque period, made during the Counter-Reformation, when spectators were encouraged to imagine themselves as immediate witnesses to the sacred dramas they saw depicted in works of art. As such, her work is alien to developments in contemporary art and to British traditions alike. The British rejection of Baroque art was cemented in the mid-nineteenth century after an attack

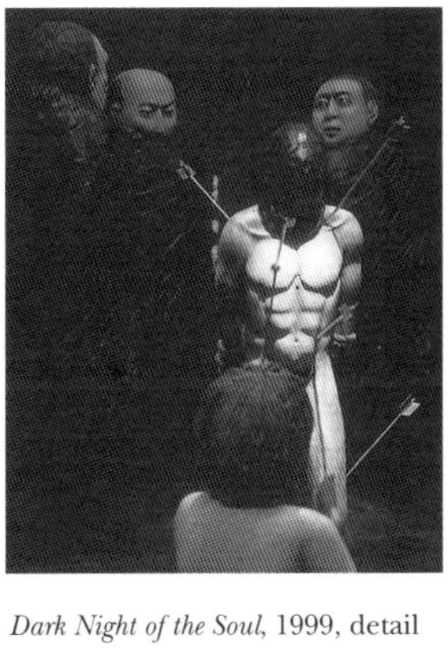

Dark Night of the Soul, 1999, detail

Dark Night of the Soul, 1999, detail

by John Ruskin. In the eighty years from 1864, the National Gallery acquired only one seventeenth-century Italian painting, which Ruskin had rendered virtually uncollectable. The explicit religiosity of such work was interpreted as a crude appeal to the emotions. Similarly, the critical response to Pacheco's work, when it made its first appearance, makes interesting reading. Although many critics were both excited and moved by the piece, there was by no means a unanimity. Martin Gayford for example, writing in the Daily Telegraph, flatly denounced the work: “A sinister X-rated version of the Muppets, twee and horrible at the same time . . . self-indulgent, artistically and emotionally, and nasty with it”. This is remarkably close to the language employed by Ruskin, when condemning the Italian Baroque: “Partly despicable, partly disgusting and partly ridiculous” he splutters, or “devoid alike, of art and decency”. The embarrassingly bared souls of Guercino and Reni were too much for Ruskin, and Gayford's reaction is coloured by that same English anti-Baroque tradition. Tom Lubbock, in the Independent, frankly admitted defeat and wrote that he suspected “that cognitive psychology can say more about what's going on here than art criticism can”.

Lubbock's response is not surprising because Pacheco's composition exploits forms that communicate psychologically and subliminally. The four log-men are arranged in a circle like prehistoric standing stones. The implication of ancient ritual is unavoidable. Furthermore they are clad in dark costumes, which are loaded with priestly connotations. The aggressive black pole in the centre, to which the victim figure is bound, thrusts itself skyward and has a totemic power relating it to objects as diverse as a Brancusi Endless Column or a traditional English maypole, whose symbolic origins have become prudishly neutered by the same culture that produced Ruskin.

Dark Night of the Soul, 1999, detail

Indeed, the sado-masochistic sexuality of Pacheco's work is a powerful part of its existence. However, it has always been part and parcel of traditional images of St. Sebastian. Some of the Old Master altarpieces that Pacheco first turned to when planning this sculpture, despite their sacred settings, were often viewed with suspicion from within the Church. While the authenticity of Sebastian's martyrdom and holiness were never in doubt, from the Renaissance onward the wisdom and motivation of publicly displaying his near naked and tormented form became questioned. Looking at certain pictures by, say, Caravaggio or Guido Reni, this is hardly surprising. There is an extraordinary altarpiece by Titian, in the church of Santa Maria dell'Salute, Venice, in which the saint, shown as young, beautiful and luxuriantly coiffured, has a strange but very apparent swelling that seems to lurk beneath his loin cloth, indicating that perversely he might be rather enjoying his martyrdom. There is no surviving documentary evidence that tells us that this particular painting was one of those criticised from within the Church but such an upfront image must have at least raised eyebrows (if nothing else). Whatever, Titian's altarpiece is part of a long tradition of sexually-dubious Sebastians that even to modern eyes seem somewhat incongruous in a sacred setting.

Dark Night of the Soul, 1999, detail

Pacheco adds her own female voice to this tradition of suspect Sebastians. Her muscular male victim is bound hard to the unambiguously upright pole. A further masculine symbol, the arrow, pierces his body in seven different places. The victim is punished for his maleness by symbols of that maleness. Furthermore, in traditional representations, Sebastian is never shown as completely naked. In the extremity of his agonies he successfully manages to retain his loin cloth which, for decency's sake, even the cruellest of his torturers would never countenance removing. Pacheco's victim figure, however, is stripped of his sacred setting. He is also stripped of his loin-cloth.

His prominent genitals rhyme with the erect pole to which he is tied. The arrows are silvered to catch the light, a device that the artist added after Gabriele Finaldi, a National Gallery curator, drew her attention to a seventeenth-century painting of the saint by Carlo Dolci, that shows him still bound but having had his arrows removed. Beams of light shine torch-like from his empty wounds, to symbolise his holiness. Dolci has replaced the inward-thrusting phallic arrows with outward shining beams of light. Pacheco's arrows, however, although taking their cue from Dolci's painting, still retain the look of things that cause suffering.

Dark Night of the Soul, 1999, detail

But for a martyr, it is a suffering that will lead to the bliss of heaven. The martyrs yearn for, indeed they passionately desire, their torments. However, it is worth remembering that mortifying the flesh and the inflicting of pain in the form of self-flagellation has enjoyed an ambiguous status within the Roman Catholic Church, its validity as a path to heaven not universally accepted. The active seeking of martyrdom has met with disapproval, as the ecstasy of suffering can often border on sexual ecstasy. One thinks of St. Theresa of Avila, whose story includes a state of sweet agonies caused by repeated thrustings of a gold-tipped arrow born by the angel who visited her. Theresa's arrow, of course, has come from heaven but the arrow is also the attribute of Eros, the classical love god whose name has entered our language with the word 'erotic'. Pacheco is not the first artist to investigate the morbid relationship between sex and religion. Bernini's beautiful sculpture of St. Theresa, finished in 1652 and still in its original Roman setting, is frankly orgasmic. Similarly, it is no coincidence that celebrated gay artist/film-maker Derek Jarman, chose to make the pierced figure of Sebastian the subject of one of his most explicitly homoerotic works, the film 'Sebastiane'.

Another source that Pacheco referred to, when investigating images of disempowered muscular males, was the photography of Robert Mapplethorpe, the celebrated or notorious (depending upon one's point of view) homosexual white American photographer who specialised in images of naked black men, often bound or hooded. These photographs were controversial for many reasons, not least their homoerotic explicitness, but more seriously, they brought up issues of exploitation and racism. Given Pacheco's Brazilian background, this provides yet another clue to the artist's multi-layered intentions. Pacheco comes from a country that was colonised by white Europeans who supported their conquest with enslaved black Africans. The indigenous population suffered dreadfully. Consequently it is hardly surprising that control and the exercise of power have been constant themes in Pacheco's work. Living in Britain since 1973, but born in Brazil in 1943, her work reflects the rich diversity of her native land, a culture steeped in a Roman Catholic tradition, with echoes of African art that bring to mind the slave trade's links with Brazil. Some of her figures have pronounced 'Aztec' features, of indigenous American origin. The priest-like figures who form the circle around the bound victim look exclusively European, especially the one who wears a belted overcoat. Although the features of the victim are concealed behind his hood, the implication is plain. The white Europeans are in charge. The figures with their African nail-heads and native American features are reduced to playing subordinate roles. Mapplethorpe's black models, as they pose naked and bound, have an identical status in relation to their white, controlling photographer.

The European settlers who were to become the dominant force in Brazil used two main weapons, violence and religion, both of which are examined in Pacheco's work. Her allusions to the art of the past, European, South American and African, are varied and deep, combined with references to modern photography and photojournalism.

Dark Night of the Soul, 1999, detail

However, Pacheco's sources are not solely confined to the visual. The title that she gives her piece, *Dark Night of the Soul,* is also the title of an important treatise by the sixteenth-century Spanish mystic, St. John of the Cross. This presents the possibility of one final and perhaps surprising interpretation of Pacheco's work. The Saint's text is written on the theme of purgation, both sensual and spiritual, that is necessary before a union with God. The title is a reference to the agonies of that purgation, through which the sufferer becomes ennobled and dignified. It is worth noting that Pacheco's victim/sufferer is still upright, his wounds do not cause him to flinch or slump to the ground. He remains firm and steadfast. The silver arrows cause him pain but through that pain they will purify him. His torments bring him to a state of grace and elevate him above the black-coated and earth-bound log-men who persecute him. They may strip him and bind him, place a hood over his head and pierce his body with arrows but it is he, the victim, who ultimately triumphs. By denying him his sight they remove him from the world of the visible and liberate him to break through to the invisible. What we, the viewers, see and what the surrounding crowd of log-men, nail-heads, arguing youths and dumb-struck women see is a tortured victim. He is the only figure without eyes but paradoxically, it is what he can see that is perhaps the true subject of this remarkable work.

▾ *Dark Night of the Soul,* 1999, detail

Ana Maria Pacheco: Dark Night of the Soul

Kathleen Adler

Dark Night of the Soul is a remarkable work, an installation of nineteen wooden figures, many of them over life-size, arranged around the kneeling figure of a masked man transfixed with arrows. The work was made during Pacheco's period as Associate Artist at the National Gallery, London, and completed in 1999. Pacheco was the fourth Associate Artist at the National Gallery, a residency that extended over more than two years, during which time she also produced paintings and prints, and opened her studio to the public and to art students on a regular basis. *Dark Night of the Soul* was first shown at the National Gallery from September 1999 to January 2000, and has subsequently toured in Britain, to Wolverhampton, Swansea, Manchester, Sheffield and Oxford.[1]

Ana Maria Pacheco was born in Goiânia, in the heart of Brazil, in 1943. Her childhood was spent in what was in many ways then an untamed place, where wild pigs ran through the streets and leopards were said to attack animals on neighbouring farms. The religious rituals of Catholicism, particularly those of Holy Week, the week before Easter, were enormously important, and Pacheco vividly remembers the candle-lit processions of the statues of the church through the dark streets of the town. The drama of this event is recreated, in a completely contemporary and individual way, in *Dark Night of the Soul*. This place of her upbringing is of immense importance – it still preoccupies her thoughts and dreams, and plays directly into her work. In an intensely Catholic place, Pacheco stood somewhat to one side, a position she has come to occupy all her life: her mother was a Protestant, and her participation in the religious life of the community was voluntary and desired, rather than imposed on her. The dark mysteries of the swamps surrounding the State of Goiás, full of huge anacondas and alligators, combine with the dark mysteries of Catholicism, nowhere more so than in *Dark Night of the Soul*.

From early on, Pacheco has viewed her native country as a place of ambivalence: "Everything looks like something it isn't", she says.[2] During her studies at the University of Goiás, where her training was in the traditions of European modernism, she found this ambivalence very marked. As she has said: "Then when you leave the building [the university] you go out to confront this landscape and ecology that has nothing to do with what you have learned . . . everything is thin, uncertain, distorted, scared and fearful like an animal hunted . . ."[3] She followed her degree in Goiás with music and education studies in Rio de Janeiro before returning to Goiás to teach. Her first breakthrough came when she was selected to represent Brazil in the São Paulo Biennale of 1971.

Lux Aeterna, 1995

In 1973 Pacheco came to London on a British Council Scholarship to the Slade School of Fine Art, London, and she has lived in Britain ever since. The ambivalence of her position in the British art world is one she relishes – she is always an outsider, both as a Brazilian woman and as a defiantly figurative artist. As she often says, to be colonised once is unfortunate, to be colonised twice is foolishness, and she has steadfastly refused colonisation by the British art establishment. The invitation to become the National Gallery's Associate Artist caused much soul searching – was this a step on the path to being an establishment figure? But in the end, her love of the collection and her excitement about the possibilities offered by being in daily close contact with it overcame these anxieties, and she moved into the Gallery's small artist's studio in 1997.

Luz Eterna, 1999, detail

Before coming to the National Gallery, Pacheco had been working on a series of

small panels on the theme of St. Sebastian. Each showed a bound man shot through with arrows, in one of ten different positions. One of these figures, kneeling and with his head covered with a hood, became the inspiration for the central figure of *Dark Night.* This figure had another origin, too, in a large drypoint of 1993, also called *Dark Night of the Soul,* which shows Odysseus bound to the mast and hooded to escape the lure of the winged sirens who taunt him. All Pacheco's work is richly overlaid with references in this way – to classical literature, to the Bible, and to her own earlier work. But Pacheco does not live in the past, she is drawn to images from cinema and photography, and two crucial elements in the formulating of the central figure of *Dark Night* were a Robert Mapplethorpe photograph of 1980 of a hooded man and a newspaper image of an executed Brazilian bandit, kneeling and savagely bound to a wooden post. Both these images were on the wall of Pacheco's studio while she developed the ideas of the sculpture.

Pacheco works very immediately with wood, first hacking out rough shapes with a chain-saw. She spends months thinking about the work, but the actual process of execution is, initially at least, very fast. She prefers not to make models, but to allow the figures to change through the carving. "I want to deal with what I don't know" is something she often says. For *Dark Night,* she did make studies because an assistant carried out the initial blocking out of the wood, and needed a guide. Following this rough carving, Pacheco works to refine areas, particularly the faces, to a high degree of finish, while allowing the bodies to retain a strong sense of the wood from which they are carved. She is not concerned about cracks developing, or about knotholes in the timber. The faces, however, are different: here, layers of gesso are applied as in her paintings, and the effect is both mask-like and as if the faces are caught in a spotlight. The eyes are inlaid onyx discs, and the teeth are an absolutely crucial Pacheco trademark. "Teeth give a very specific look to a face, because people's teeth are always different . . . The look of the teeth can change a face enormously."[4] The teeth serve both to individualise the figures, and to give them a connection to the traditions of West African tribal masks, with their resonances in the history of colonial Brazil – more slaves came to Brazil from Africa than to any other country. The links to African art often continue in the hair of the figures: the wood is burned with a blowtorch, and nails are often inserted. Intense colours are applied to areas like the lips and cheeks using cotton buds, and this colouring recalls another tradition, the tradition of Brazilian Baroque polychrome sculpture. In that sculpture, too, the faces are strikingly white, an artifice in a country so multi-ethnic, in which whiteness is the exception, not the rule.

Pacheco's links to this tradition of polychrome Baroque sculpture are strong. She loves the richness of its iconography, and is drawn to the violence of much of the imagery. A favourite motif for her is the severed head, sometimes deliberately that of St. John the Baptist, sometimes linked to Brazilian bandits and public executions. The work of the sculptor O Aleijadinho (Antônio Francisco Lisboa), dating from the last years of the eighteenth century and the first years of the nineteenth century, has powerfully affected her. His works were carved in cedarwood, with glass eyes. The most important of his works are at Congonhas, where *The Stations of the Cross* consists of more than sixty figures. Their polychromy was restored in the 1950s, giving them back their full dramatic impact. Pacheco takes this tradition and reworks it, and the strength and drama of these sculptural installations is a force in the conception of *Dark Night of the Soul.*

Drama is always at the heart of Pacheco's work, never more so than in *Dark Night.* She totally resists the concept of 'cool', wanting instead to create deep emotional

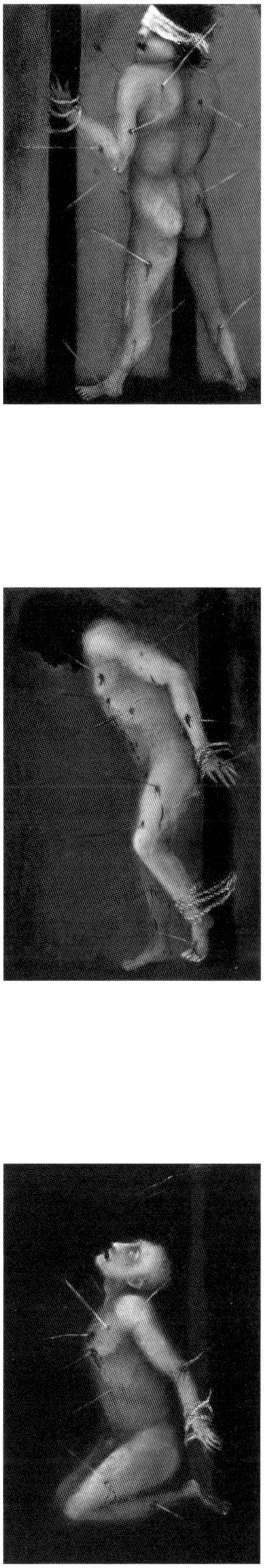

Untitled, 1996, detail of three panels

Dark Night of the Soul, 1999, detail

responses in the viewers, and is never afraid to tap into themes of death, torture, guilt and culpability. This nonplussed some British art critics when the work was shown at the National Gallery. Their response was very much that of the writer and critic John Ruskin to Baroque art in another century: a shrinking away from the excess and intensity of such Catholic art.

What is the subject of the work? Although the hooded and bound figure with the silvered arrows piercing his body is associated with St. Sebastian, Pacheco resisted naming the piece in this way. St. Sebastian was a Roman archer, in the service of the Emperor Diocletian, who converted to Christianity. In punishment, the Emperor ordered him to be shot by his fellow archers. Traditionally, the figure of St. Sebastian usually stands, and his head is always visible. He is often a somewhat effete youth. Pacheco has studied many examples of Sebastian imagery, particularly the National Gallery's great altarpiece by the brothers Pollaiuolo, dating from the 1470s, but her figure is more than a specific Christian saint. She chose the title, *Dark Night of the Soul*, taken from the writings of the Spanish mystic St. John of the Cross, to suggest a struggle deep inside oneself, rather than the visible martyrdom of St. Sebastian, and this is what the other figures in the group, as well as the main figure, convey.

The four men who surround the Sebastian figure are over life-size, their bodies undifferentiated, still very much suggesting the tree trunks from which they were hewn. Pacheco calls them the 'conspiratorial figures' and the suggestion that they are complicit in the situation in which the kneeling figure finds himself is strong. But unlike the archers in traditional representations of St. Sebastian, there is no indication that they have actually shot and bound him. The relationship of the other figures to the kneeling figure is equally complex and ambivalent. The grouping of the woman holding a child, the naked child, and the kneeling woman may at one level represent innocence, but the woman with the child seems enthralled by what is in front of her. The child on her hip, on the other hand, is linked only to her mother. The group of men whom Pacheco calls the 'thugs', behind the kneeling figure, appear to be arguing about what they see, almost ready to come to blows, while the woman next to them has her hand to her mouth in a gesture of shock or apprehension. This expression occurs often in Pacheco's work, both in sculpture and in paintings.[5] One of the most puzzling figures is the large isolated figure of a woman, who at first seems menacing, severe and grim. Protracted looking suggests another reading: that she is deeply distressed, and questioning her position in this event. This figure's body reveals the full contradictoriness of Pacheco's technique: on the one hand it is impossible to avoid discussing these figures as if they are people; on the other hand no attempt is made to render them in a manner which suggests anything other than their woodenness. This torso has deep splits in the wood, and the chisel marks of the making are strongly in evidence, as is the grain of the wood.[6] But the split can also be viewed as the split in the woman's response to the scene. And the deep red of the dress is the colour of blood, the split in the wood an open wound.

Dark Night of the Soul, 1999, detail

Rough-hewn wood is set against precise detail. One of the group of three arguing men has a shoelace that is meant to be unfastened – although visitors and gallery security staff seem to ensure that it is retied daily. Shoes and boots are a preoccupation of Pacheco's and they are meticulously rendered, as are details such as the toggle fastening of a hooded top, or the neck of a sweater. Pacheco was particularly concerned to contrast the roughness of the other figures against the smooth bodied, strongly muscled naked kneeling figure. The seven arrows which pierce the body are silvered, their fineness a striking contrast to the coarseness of the rope which binds him. These arrows can be detached, and their perfection is violently at odds with their function, their tips penetrating the body in a series of bruised holes. The silver leaf technique was less challenging than obtaining the exactly correct rope. Hemp ropes like this are no longer made, and it was a butcher's shop which provided the solution, a rope that had been used to hang bloody carcasses from ceiling hooks and so was appropriate both in itself and in the function it had previously served. Pacheco jokes that one day this rope will have to be returned, it has only been loaned to her. The trunk to which the rope is fastened is a cut-off telegraph pole, another aspect of the inventiveness which characterises the piece, and another instance of Pacheco's clear vision of how each part of the whole must function. Different woods were used: Pacheco's preferred timber, lime, a homage to the limewood sculpture of Central Europe in the fourteenth and fifteenth centuries, was difficult to obtain and a source was only found late in the production of the piece. One of the invisible qualities of the work is that it still smells faintly of different woods, an effect that was very marked in the months of its production, and one which added to the complex relationship between representation and realism.

Dark Night of the Soul, 1999, detail

From the outset, how the work would be displayed and lit was a prime consideration. Pacheco wants more than passive viewing from her audiences. She wants us to enter a space that is not ours, and to lose certainty about that space and our position in it.[7] You cannot just stand outside this sculpture, it demands of you that you enter it. Pacheco wants it to invade our space, to force us to reconsider ourselves in relation to the figures of the sculpture. The base is crucial in establishing the continuity of the piece, and in linking the figures, but it is also the stage on which both sculpted figures and spectators engage. From the darkness emerge spotlit figures, their faces strangely white and smooth, some of them much larger than we are, against which we measure ourselves and our own thoughts. Pacheco says that everyone reads this work according to what they bring with them, and while that must be true of our experience of all art, it is powerfully palpable here, often evoking strong reactions on the part of viewers. In the National Gallery, one woman told us, tears streaming down her face, that it had evoked her own experiences as a child in Nazi-occupied Holland, her own 'dark night of the soul'. Others were struck dumb with amazement – teenage girls stopped giggling, small children were fascinated by the children in the group.

Dark Night of the Soul, 1999, detail

One of the most compelling effects of the sculpture, which never fails and never fails to amaze, is that these figures, which are not individually particularly lifelike, seem to move, and as viewers move, there is an intense sense that these wooden objects have somehow moved too. This is always a shock – it is against all reason that we should experience this. The transformation of wooden sculpture to living presence is magical, and its recurrence, over and over again, is always startling. Pacheco says that the figures still do this to her: she turns her back and is convinced that a figure has moved. The ability to defy the commonplace or commonsensical has always been a feature of Pacheco's work, which explores the unfamiliar, the unknown, and the uncharted territories of the subconscious. But she is not a surrealist, and neither is she a representative of 'Latin American magic realism'. Pacheco despises the thinking that positions all the different cultures of South America as 'Latin American' as much as she has contempt for the idea of 'magic realism' as a label for the visual arts. Seeking to label her work is always doomed to failure, and worse, to misunderstanding its subtlety and complexity. As the poet George Szirtes has written: "We play these games of association and form as if they were a riddle waiting for some Oedipal answer, and it is all we are going to get. Provisional riddles have provisional solutions. The final riddles we don't talk about."[8]

Dark Night of the Soul, 1999, detail

Pacheco likes to say: "I come from a colonial country, a mixture of cultures that forms a very thick soup, I don't carry the baggage of someone born in Europe."[9]

The 'thick soup' of Pacheco's position as a Brazilian artist based in Britain, working with a myriad of references, densely intertwined and complex, subtle and challenging, has nowhere been more fully resolved than in this sculpture, *Dark Night of the Soul.* To enter it is to experience another world, and to engage more fully with our own deepest feelings and emotions.

Notes

1 During Ana Maria Pacheco's stay at the National Gallery, I was privileged to see the development of this piece from the outset, and to have almost daily conversations with her. Remarkably, this Brazilian acquired a taste for Earl Grey tea, and my colleague Colin Wiggins and I spent many hours with her talking about her work. This was an enormous honour and pleasure and I apologise to Ana if I have misquoted her at any point. Colin Wiggins devised and runs the National Gallery's programme of work with contemporary artists, and he worked extremely closely with Ana during the period of her being Associate Artist. I am also grateful to Susan and Bernard Pratt of Pratt Contemporary Art.

2 Quotations from Pacheco are from many conversations, discussions with students, public lectures. This last comment was made during a conversation with Colin Wiggins at the opening of her exhibition at the Ashmolean Museum, 5 July 2001.

3 Ian Starsmore, *'Inventing the Black Powder': Art and Education*, Pratt Contemporary Art, Sevenoaks, 1989.

4 Ana Maria Pacheco in conversation with Colin Wiggins, *Ana Maria Pacheco in the National Gallery*, National Gallery Publications Limited, 1999, p. 47.

5 For example, in the painting *In Illo Tempore X* of 1994, or in *Memória Roubada IV* of 1992. See *Ana Maria Pacheco in the National Gallery*, pp. 22-3.

6 Although these marks of making are so in evidence in the sculpture, Pacheco prefers the surface of her paintings to be entirely smooth, without any of the gestural qualities that she associates with the art of male painters.

7 Ana Maria Pacheco in conversation with Colin Wiggins, Ashmolean Museum, Oxford, 5 July 2001.

8 Szirtes wrote this of *Requiem* (1986-95) in a sheet accompanying its exhibition. Quoted in *Ana Maria Pacheco in the National Gallery*, p.10.

9 *Ana Maria Pacheco in the National Gallery*, National Gallery Publications Limited, 1999. p. 25.

Flowing to the Unknown: Streams of Change, Rivers of Communion

Nicolau Sevcenko

When I first set eyes on Orpheus and Eurydice (*Hades I*, oil pastel, 1998) by Ana Maria Pacheco, I felt one of those rare moments of revelation, such as happens when a large collection of fragments suddenly takes on a clear, consistent order. The fragments were the works that this many-faceted artist untiringly creates and engenders. There were her drawings, transformed into engravings, which in turn became paintings, themselves later metamorphosed into sculptures which set off more sketches and drawings, and so on. From time to time, as I contemplated this vast gallery of enigmatic figures, elusive settings and dead-end situations, my growing fascination gradually became a pressing need to find some chain of meaning that might link this teeming but silent world, shut off in itself and perturbing in its mystery.

The image shows Orpheus, in Charon's boat, at the fatal moment when his forbidden gaze rests on Eurydice, and he is at once penetrated by her irresistible beauty and suddenly aware of the tragic consequences of his urge to see. Eurydice, unmoved by her lover's passionate ordeal and by his terror, presents him with the majestic calm of her last look. Despite the intensity of the drama, the scene is bathed in a lyrical innocence. The figures radiate with a slightly iridescent luminosity, beneath the gloomy shades of Hades; one can feel the cold of the waters of the Styx, but there is no way of hearing the trembling pulsation, the terrified breathing, or the last cry exchanged between the two lovers. Silence suspends the senses. Do we really understand everything that happens in that moment?

This doubt makes us look again. Only then do we see that the artist has reformulated the whole basis of the myth. In the original version they are walking, with Orpheus in front, and Eurydice carefully following in his footsteps along the rough, winding, monster-infested paths of Hades. He knew the way, because that was how he had got in. It was she who had been carried by Charon's boat in the final crossing of the Styx. Ana Maria Pacheco's Eurydice shows none of the characteristics of a Greek maiden. Her features, the formal refinement of her clothing, the ornaments she wears, her ritual veil and hieratic posture suggest rather a Moorish lady, or the Afro-Brazilian goddess *Yemanjá*.[1] The boat does not look Greek; it could be a native Brazilian pirogue or canoe. The Charon in this image is not the old man who ferried the dead, but a mischievous version of Hermes the trickster, the god of cunning, of illusions and crossroads. What is he doing there? What are they all doing on the river? In the final analysis, is it the tormented Orpheus that is looking at Eurydice, or is it she, calm, steady and assured, who looks at him? Who is sacrificing whom? What myth is this? What's going on here?

In a trice, everything is changed. The world dissolves beneath our feet, and we are suspended over an unexplored abyss. That is what Ana Maria Pacheco's visual alchemy does. It makes the familiar look strange, and sets up disconcertingly intimate links with something that is totally foreign. This is the so-called Unheimlich, the uncanny, the subject of one of Freud's most famous essays, on Hoffman's tales. But it is also more than that, because Ana Maria Pacheco has an enviable stock of erudition, so that when she moves between different areas of meaning, her journey highlights the cultural contexts and references in the visual and narrative traditions that interact in her oeuvre. Therefore, her works bring imaginary projections (in the Freudian sense) into play, which attach themselves to archaic mythical contents, in an attempt to confront historical tensions of the greatest importance in our own world. In reality,

Overleaf: *Hades I*, 1998 ▸

her work is a process.

Her reformulation of the myth of Orpheus and Eurydice brought to my mind the remarkable affinity between her artistic project and the thought of Heraclitus, the most inspired of the pre-Socratic philosophers. He said: "if we do not expect the unexpected we will not discover it, since it is not to be searched out and is difficult to comprehend". Like Ana Maria, Heraclitus communicated by means of enigmas, and like her, he thought that "all things are in process and nothing stays still; we cannot step twice into the same river".[2]

As is well known, the river was Heraclitus' principal metaphor. The probable reason for this was that his native city, Ephesus in Asia Minor, owed its great prosperity to the river Caÿster, and to its port on the Aegean Sea, which made it the most important entrepôt for mercantile and symbolic exchange between several worlds: the Persian empire to the east, Thrace and Greece to the west, the Caucasus and the Black Sea to the north, and, to the south, Egypt and the Semitic peoples. The river was no mere rhetorical figure for Heraclitus; he really thought and felt as if he were the river itself. "New and different waters flow around those who step into the same river. It disperses and comes together . . . flows in and out . . . towards us and away."

For Ana Maria Pacheco too, the river is not just a symbol. Her art is a continual, unpredictable flux, in which usually separate elements come into contact and, at the same time, solid things dissolve. She comes from Goiás, deep in the Brazilian interior. The Portuguese who colonised Brazil never dared to penetrate the thick jungle of the backlands, keeping close to the coasts and to the security of the ships that linked them to Europe. But Brazil is above all characterised by its extraordinary network of rivers, which covers every region of the country. As the Indians knew, in the dense jungles, the only possible roads are the rivers, and whoever controls them will also dominate the land. Thus, it was the 'mamelucos', the offspring of poor colonists and the Indian women of the Jesuit missions, who ended up conquering the Brazilian interior, always moving along the rivers. It was they who gave origin to Goiás, one of several settlements in the backlands. Eventually, they came across the gold and diamonds that attracted colonists and black slaves into the interior. In this atmosphere of cultural fusion between Indians, blacks, whites and mestizos of all shades, there flourished the cultural synthesis that was the Baroque.

Ana Maria Pacheco comes from this world of rivers, this great human and cultural flux. Her art is the river, but it is also the boat, the boatman, the crew, the travellers and castaways, and the monsters that lurk in the waters. In every harbour, familiar people disembark, and new, unfamiliar figures come on board. Everyone is accepted, they all have something to teach us; as Heraclitus says, "dogs [are the ones that] bark at strangers". The journey continues. There is no ultimate destination; crossing the sea is a destiny in its own right, and "things are directed through all things", according to the philosopher of Ephesus. The master of the Caÿster river flows alongside the artist from the river Paranaíba, joined across continents and time.

This conception of a crossing as a destiny is also one of the foundations of Afro-Brazilian culture. Exiled from Africa by a journey in a 'tumbeiro' [a slave-ship, or literally 'tomb-ship'], the blacks represented their destiny as a *kalunga*, the passage from the motherland to a land of punishment; they move between a present suffering and a distant communion, across the gap between the human condition and possession by the divine power of the *orixá*.[3] Their art expresses an instinctive aversion to the world of devils to which they have been condemned, and against which they struggle, using masks, grotesque figureheads, statuettes, dolls and allegories, reminiscent of African *bimbi* and *knisi*. This is the art of anamorphosis, of wood burnt and pierced full of nails, an art that repels the onlooker, with its menacing teeth, and which produces the unspeakable discomfort of Ana Maria Pacheco's art. It is also the art of *metaxy* or 'in-betweenness' of Heraclitus, who seems to be speaking of her when he talks of "[t]he raving Sibyl, [who], through the god, utters sombre, unembellished, unperfumed sayings, reaching over a thousand years with her voice".

This wandering between the times, cultures and dilemmas that afflict the present makes Ana Maria's art particularly appropriate to this transition into the twenty-first century. In her continual voyage, she shows up hubris, the self-centred, intolerant arrogance of power, as the dark force, the pestilent sphinx that devastates the pluralist societies of the contemporary world. More than once she finds herself in harmony with Heraclitus, for whom "overweening pride is the sacred disease". The mystery omnipresent in her works also finds expression in the thought of the Greek master, for whom "a hidden connection is stronger than an apparent one". For anyone made uncomfortable by Ana Maria Pacheco's insistence on dealing with tense, conflict-ridden situations, the philosopher also has a retort: "[t]hey do not apprehend how being in conflict it still agrees with itself; there is an opposing coherence, as in the tensions of the bow and the lyre". And of course, with the lyre, we come back to the theme of Orpheus; and to the wonderment that gave rise to this text.

Translated by John Gledson

Notes

1 *Yemanjá*, feminine deity in the African cult of Ioruba; in Brazil she is the 'Queen' of the seas.
2 *Remembering Heraclitus, the philosopher of riddles*, Richard Geldard, Floris Books, Edinburgh, 2000.
3 *Orixá*: deity from the Nagô Cult.

For Ana, my sister, my friend

John Clark

He whose heart has been washed
will go through fire without turning;
he will ascend the great mountain without homesickness;
I did not get such a spirit
since my heart is only half flayed.

from *Prayer* by Sorley Maclean [1]

For me Ana is someone very close, an artist, and the bearer of cultural traces. Let me take the last element first, since it is a measure of her stature that whatever the concreteness personal exchange, she has always stimulated me to think of broader matters. Please allow me to meander slightly towards showing what that means.

'Brazil' is a kind of cultural 'other' for me, to which I come via a what may be an unusual route, that of understanding Asia, and also of coming to terms with slavery and later horrors. I am a scholar of chiefly modern Asian art and for many Europeans I suppose the 'East' is, even now, all a bit of a mystery, a fantasised, invented place for exoticising and exploiting, in the manner for which the hermeneutic stereotype of 'Orientalism' so beguilingly – if deceptively – fits. I have always found the sanctimonious ease by which this ideogram allows the decipherment of slippery meanings in cross-cultural contact hard to accept, even under a colonial order or its contemporary residues. I am not really able to conceive of cultures not my own as 'other' since I knew Chinese families quite well when I was an adolescent and had African friends at University. The notion that my knowledge of them was screened by some exoticised system of representations after a certain point was inaccurate if not wrong. To think that Africans were culturally 'different', or that Asian languages were intractably 'difficult' and alienating seemed plain silly after a little effort and concentrated exposure showed the languages could be learned and the cultures in many ways assimilated to.

But Latin America was a different matter. The savageries of European conquest followed by the blinding cruelties of slavery, all were an echo of something buried in European history but somehow distant, incommensurable. It was like the gap between Anglican low-church sermons on black souls being all equal in the sight of God, and the child's shrieking nightmare of the slave shackles I had seen in the Wilberforce Museum aged six or seven. The impression of horror was reinforced for it being ritually sited in time and place, one early 1950s Christmas shopping visit across the mist-shrouded Humber on a ferry to Hull. 'We did this?'

The child asks how we can be complicit in an evil we did not do, but the adult sense of this begins in the self-critique of one's own culture or more broadly of civilisation. In my case, the notion that we were all responsible for the ultimate nastiness of humankind – the word 'evil' seems inadequate – was later brought to his teenage children by my father, a rather conservative, upwardly mobile engineer. His own father had been a goodly Christian man who radiated love to all who knew him, but who had fought for three months in the sewers of Ypres. So far as is known he *never* spoke of this experience to anyone. Like many of his generation, I imagine the shadow of complicity in a great wrong hung over his life. Later our own father gave us to know, after a visit in 1959 to the by then museified remains of Dachau, that even English soldiers in 1945 had thought European civilisation itself, and not just Germany

Between Mitcham and Croydon, The Heritage of the Aged, 1977.
◂ detail

The Banquet I, 1978

The Banquet II, 1978

or its culture, was the real perpetrator of the Holocaust.

Latin America, from conquistadors, the 'conversion of the Indians', to the military dictatorships of the 1960s and 1970s, seemed like one continuous zone where this human nastiness had worked itself out, away from the eyes of history, or at least was only dimly perceived by Northern Europeans of average Protestant background. The first thing I learned from Ana was, I suppose, that all this dream of heat and fear was the projection of distance and ignorance, and that it could be understood in human lives and symbols as not so very far away at all from British experience, nor distant from the self-critique of civilisation, like my father's.

This is peculiarly evident in two prints she did at Croydon where I had come to work on painting for a year: *Between Mitcham and Croydon – The Heritage of the Aged*, 1977, and *The Banquet*, 1978. In the former, old women seem to be hanging around at a bus stop chattering out the last years of their lives with an animate malevolence, blaming the others. But they are also liminal figures, consumed by their own antipathies as much as they project them. What might appear ostensibly as a hard look at the night which will envelop us all, becomes a meditation on human spiritual weakness and the sometimes perverse expressions of this inward knowledge. They are not quite absorbed into a specific mythological representation, The Furies, but the viewer senses this is on the verge of a symbolic and not just a quotidian order.

In the latter, the masked faces seem about to devour the onlooker as much as each other. Anthropophagy, as I was later to become aware, has since the 1920s been a recurrent topos in Brazilian modernist art and literature, a discourse of counter-absorption on the terms of the local imaginary of cultural forms from the colonial centre. In a more explicit symbolic order the mask is only one step away from allegory, a kind of all-body mask. Here Ana points to a continuing preoccupation with the *figure*, a profoundly modern mode of representational abstraction, where figuration is an extended discursial body of types that stands for other forces which could be named and brought into play by the device of attributing them to pre-existing mythological or literary identities. We could easily look for and find in Ana's work distant Brazilian antecedents for these figures and situations, but they are also found here and now, in daily Northern European lives far from Brazilian night.

The imaginary which links Ana's *figures* is not a casuistical ordering of a Jesuit kind, nor its opposite, a simplistic anti-clerical diatribe. It is a profoundly secular and polysemic re-positioning of image types, literary, religious, and mythic naming systems, and of the forces they conjure up. If sometimes inclining to that ambivalent art, magic, or even to the occult, Ana's work also echoes simpler oppositions conceived as Catholic / Protestant, speaking indirectly to God via the priest (the work) as against directly via the written inspiration of God's word (the naming of the work). I had always naively thought of Brazil as a profoundly Roman Catholic country, but whilst Ana's father was a Catholic, her mother was a Protestant and Ana cannot be conceived as having any nameable religion, except perhaps a rather fatalistic love of humanity and its arts. Neither does she come from the narrow Brazilian 'coast' with its by turns sugary or cynical indifferences, but from the limitless, hard 'interior', close to the dedicated lust for gold and land, to Indian peoples the subject of massacres in her own lifetime and not just in some distant pre-slavery past.

Indeed, the past may have a way of allowing a glimpse of its unfamiliar meanings in such centres distant from the time and geography of an 'original' locale. Many people in her family have an 'Arab' look. 'Muslims', 'Jews' and 'Arabs' could be enslaved in the Portuguese kingdoms because they were not 'Christian', and some of their Jewish Arab descendants were concentrated in a part of Brazil occupied by the Dutch. From this a quite different, potential sensibility appears as if out of time and place. It is ultimately an a-theist tolerance, but one which by historically forced hybridity is more magnanimous of magical polytheism than any occupying 'Christianity' could be. Significantly, Ana recently confessed Arabic is one language she might still like to learn.

Another gap with Brazilian historical realities was closed for me by her indicating the late eighteenth-century Brazilian Baroque sculptor and architect Alejadinho, whose works stem from a time the gold mining and slave owning elite felt more prosperous and civilised than the Portuguese in Europe. The almost self-mocking richness and elaboration of his forms, hybrid as he also was by ethnic origin, point to the tying of the artist-craftsman to a certain puffed-up pretension of the Brazilian rulers which scarcely admitted criticism from beneath. Already Alejadinho's work carries premonitions of that presumed indulgence of the artist by the audience which is found in the late nineteenth-century sardonic writing of Machado de Assis. It indicates a very small, and at times stiflingly suffocating space for the artist to work either as a social critic, or with the formal modalities of an art. I sometimes think Ana's great love of music, and of certain interpretations of Bach, like Tureck's for example, are a kind of formalised resistance to such pretence, one founded in part on piano training as a child, but also on an adult knowledge of what lies on the other side when the veneer of cultural legitimacy turns to brute domination.

An Australian friend once said, apropos of recent racist politics, that the problem with 'white civilisation' in Queensland was that it was rather thin. The thought recently returned as Ana casually mentioned that when she had taught art in high school at the time of the generals her name had been put on the list of those for 'interrogation', but only 'by mistake'. It was removed at the last moment through the efforts of a sympathetic principal. Torture or even death could turn on the triviality of denunciation through professional jealousy, and safety could depend on mere personal sympathy. The confluence of broader and particular individual histories comes strangely clear. Humanity can always be implicated in wider horrors, even for those who do not commit them, but in the twentieth century particular humans we know could also be just a telephone call away from becoming a victim.

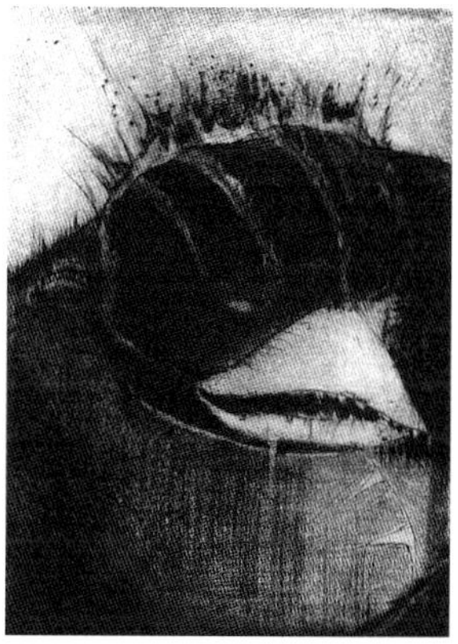

This Time they Came to Stay, 1978

Others will have noticed the percussive qualities of Ana's touch, just like a pianist. I first met her in 1977 coming out of the room in the printing studio with the heat treatment ovens for applying aquatint to etching plates. She had a very ink-stained T-shirt on and was doing what I can only describe as a kind of dance in the air with the plate at the end of her robust but deftly firm fingertips. In this first moment of encounter I sensed, if only later understood, her resilience and determination with the artistic process. She was unafraid to repeat and repeat a process or the drawing of a particular image until it became adequate for her purposes. She was able to carry this forward often under gruelling personal circumstances, including living in a Tudor barn through the rigours of a Kent winter, carving with gloves on against nearly sub-zero temperatures inside. Some may wonder why Ana went through many of the everyday sufferings of the artist in Britain when she might have returned to Brazil and lived a good life as a recognised artist or teacher. True, her world in Britain was compensated in part by the wide circle of friends she was able to make in music and art, some of whom were old European refugees from Nazism, or their children. I suppose the answer may be that the difficulties of life for a time in the late 1970s and early 1980s were preferable to the artistic asphyxiation she might expect to have experienced in Brazil.

This Time they Came to Stay, 1978

Despite Ana's longstanding artistic achievement and her more recent, tangible

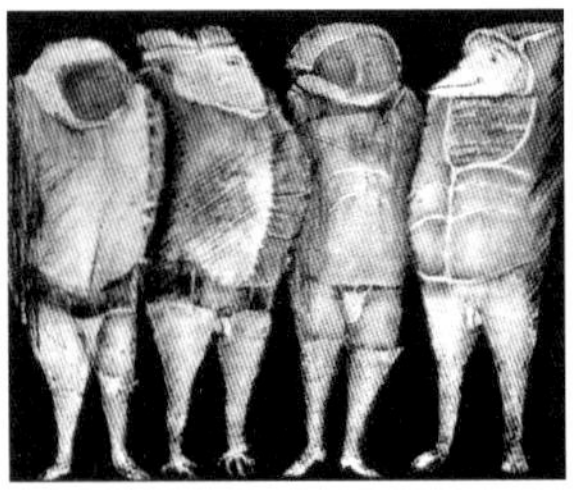

Daemoni Vera Dicenti Non Est Credendum, 1978

social recognition via the Residency at the National Gallery in London, I suspect that the difficulty in her work is also what makes it appeal to a wide public beyond her quite specific audience in the art world. She does not readily engage with striking a position and her aesthetic concerns the marking of states of grace or the fall from it. The work is of beauty and truth itself. The British have not always been known to others, even to themselves, as having a rich visual culture. Perhaps this popular recognition of Ana's work might indicate another evaluation. In a time when fashion has moved from being a parasite on art, to art having become the parasite of fashion – whatever the role of advertising magnates in setting canons of taste – her work is peculiarly, and one might think deliberately unmediatisable. Ana's work is like that she admires of Bill Viola which resists simple dissemination via images, despite its technical sophistication. She works hard on forms because the art of forms is hard. We should be glad someone still knows how to work at carving them.

Notes

1 Somhairle McGill-Eain, *O Choille gu Bearradh* / Sorley Maclean, *From Wood to Ridge, Collected Poems in Gaelic with English Translation*, Manchester & Edinburgh, Carcanet/Birlinn, 1999.

Transformations

Colin Wiggins

This set of pastel drawings, *Transformations*, is the first project to have been completed by Ana Maria Pacheco in her studio at the National Gallery. Born in Brazil in 1943 and resident in England since 1973, Ana Maria Pacheco arrived at the gallery in April 1997, as the fourth National Gallery Associate Artist. It is planned to hold an exhibition of the work she produces for this scheme at the Gallery in the autumn of 1999. Significantly, she is the first non-European to be invited to take up this position.

Transformations II, 1997

The source material for this new work is Ovid's *Metamorphoses*, a text that has provided fertile ground for artists since its rediscovery during the Renaissance. These familiar tales of transformations become themselves transformed, as Ovid's Classical stories meet a culture from another continent.

As Associate Artist at the National Gallery, Pacheco's brief is to make work inspired by its collection, which is of course in a solely European tradition, a tradition that includes Ovid's poetry. Yet the trappings of Classicism, which are so closely associated with the Greek and Roman myths, have gone. In their place is darkness, enchantment and exoticism. The clear Mediterranean light that usually provides the setting for representations of these stories is replaced with something altogether different. Stories we thought could no longer surprise us become unfamiliar and threatening.

Transformations IV, 1997

Pacheco's method of relating her work to the art of the past is not simply by appropriating compositions or motifs. Rather, it is by immersing herself in its subject matter. This is not, however, to rule out unconscious quotation. The group of animal-headed figures on the right of *Transformations IV*, for example, with their translucent and columnar white costumes, are strongly reminiscent of the celebrated choir of angels in Piero della Francesca's Nativity. When this was pointed out to the artist, she expressed first of all surprise, then agreement. Viewers of these new drawings will find their own examples of such subliminal borrowings, which are an inevitable consequence of day-to-day contact with the Old Masters. One deliberate reference is to *The Wilton Diptych*, whose white hind becomes the wounded deer in *Transformations V*. The only other direct quote that Pacheco admits to is the labyrinth in *Transformations I & II*. This, though, is not taken from a painting in the National Gallery's collection but from a rather grim brick courtyard immediately outside her studio. Even her humdrum daily surroundings become transformed, absorbed into her mythic world.

Transformations III, 1997

Although these new pictures are independent works in their own right, they are also preparations for an ambitious set of paintings and sculptures that Pacheco plans to start work on in the near future, as part of her involvement with the National Gallery. The deep psychological dramas and the compositional complexities in these drawings have given her the momentum to delve into two subjects deeply rooted in the past, The Temptation of St. Anthony and The Martyrdom of St. Sebastian.

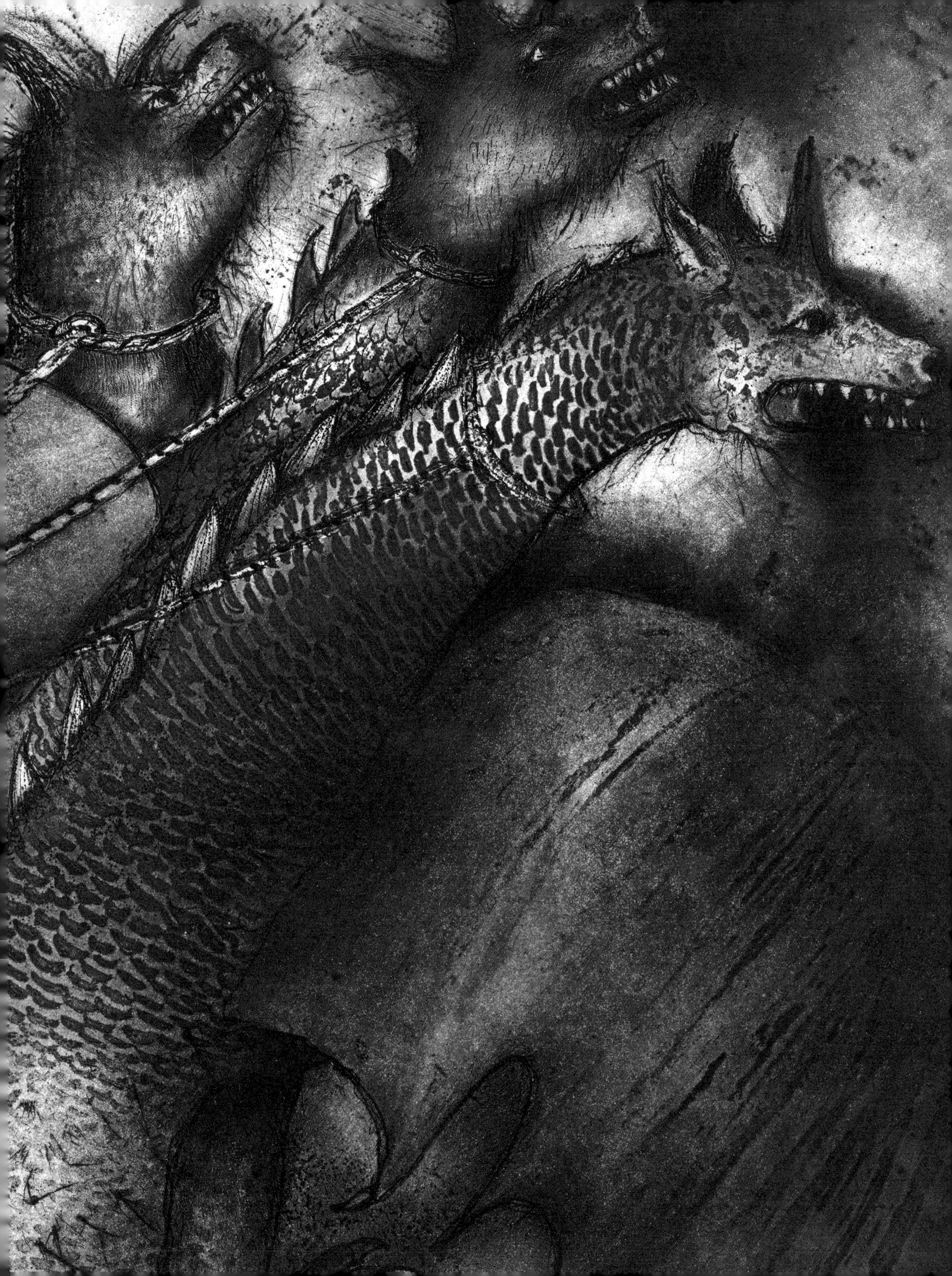

Ana Maria Pacheco's Metamorphoses

Amanda Hopkinson

Our earliest art bears witness to our deeply ambivalent relationship with the rest of the living world. Did our ancestors paint the caves of Altamira and Lascaux with the beasts they wished to worship or to dominate? Perhaps it was simply an early visual record of how humans use eating as a means of ingesting the laudable attributes of the creatures we honour. It is equally a part of religious practice, including Christianity's sacrament of the Eucharist. As is its converse, that of animals transforming themselves into humans or gods, to put our faith and fidelity to the test. In *The Banquet* (1985) Ana Maria Pacheco has already given us the carving of a man on the trencher prepared to be carved up, a subject as resonant with the tortures of the military dictators who had seized power in her home country before she left, as of its legends of cannibalism, and in particular the ingestion of the brains of the powerful among the 'natives'.

In this new series of prints Pacheco straddles the religious, mythic and popular, inevitably emphasising the commonality of all three in the invocation of sacrifice, transformation and consumption. In a Brazilian folk tale, a medicine man turns a tribesman into a tapir who is killed and eaten. The women are angry and jump into the river, changing into fishes. *Tales of Transformations 3* depicts how they finally agree to permit their men to fish them back again as women, a moral as sound as any in Aesop, curiously replacing cunning with the virtue of forgiveness. The drypoint is as deliberately simple and humorous as a *folheto*,[1] the woman's arms flailing as she splashes through her metamorphosis.

Tales of Transformations 1-3, 1998

It's a virtue that found little favour with classical Mediterranean civilisation. How different to Circe's fury at the men she transforms into swine emerging, in Ana Maria Pacheco's version (*Tales of Transformations II*), to survey them in smug triumph. Vengeance is the basis of so many Greek legends that Ovid's *Metamorphoses* at times seem like recitals of rage and fear so incandescent that transformation is their one release. Here Medea drives the great chariot drawn by three dragons (*Tales of Transformations I*). Eurydice looks downcast from beneath her haze of purple veils as Orpheus is here drawn from her by a boat rowed by Charon (*Tales of Transformations IV*). By working always from dark into light, Ana Maria Pacheco allows the stars spangling the velvet sky between the cypresses an element of surprise, like the gold leaf which barely tinges the lance and antlers of the white hart (*Tales of Transformations III*). Here the legend anticipates its Christian version in which St Hubert (or, by other accounts, St Eustace) was cured of going hunting on a Good Friday when the crucifix appeared shining between a white stag's antlers, as in Pisanello's *The Vision of St Eustace* in London's National Gallery.

As the National Gallery's current Associate Artist, Ana Maria Pacheco cites Pollaiuolo's St. Sebastian as the only one to have had an influence among all the examples the gallery possesses. Gombrich calls Pollaiuolo's six executioners "both vigorous and lifelike", and it is these qualities which most inform the work of Pacheco's Brazilian compatriots, the high Baroque sculptors O Aleijadinho ('The Little Cripple') and Veiga Valle (from her home state of Goiás). Each heavily invokes the Mysteries through the everyday, their human-sized statues so lifelike as to resemble actors in medieval morality plays. (And, in *The Longest Journey*, Ana Maria Pacheco has already used a real boat as it would have been taken for a *Chegança*, one of four 'tableaux vivants' traditionally displayed before churches during Holy Week.) Either

Tales of Transformations II, 1997-8

◂ *Tales of Transformations I*, detail

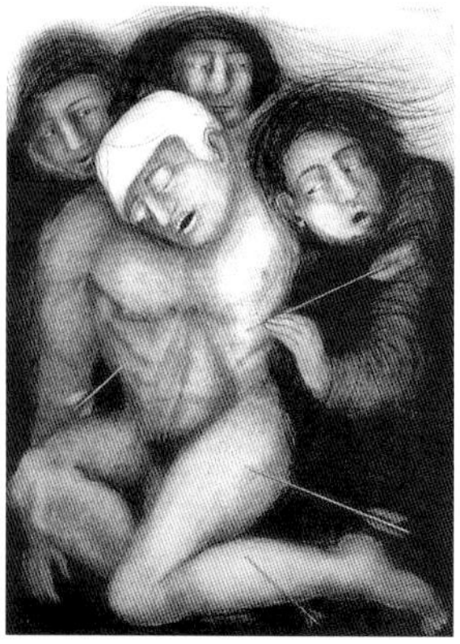

Study for St. Sebastian I, 1998

Study for St. Sebastian II, 1998

way, the medieval and Baroque win out over Classicism or Modernism, the other art-forms most vying for prominence.

Ana Maria Pacheco names three equally surprising sources for these new series. Specifically, *Study for St Sebastian I & II* derives a prize-winning press portrait of a judicially executed Brazilian bandit, garrotted against a tree stump and shot through the side, blood streaming as though from Christ's side on a processional crucifix. While familiar with the biblical inspiration rampant in our National Gallery, Pacheco was not anticipating the copious references to Ovid's *Metamorphoses.* Since all her pictures tell stories, there is no surprise in finding again a triumph of a verbal over a visual starting point.

Back to Ana Maria Pacheco's roots deep in the Brazilian interior. Animal/animist fables have long been part of an oral tradition. While many of African origin have entered the common canon through school editions (rather as we absorbed *Brer Rabbit* and *Anansi Spider* ones), those of indigenous ('indian') origin have lacked a printed outlet. Once again, the pleasure is also in making connections – between the grandmother and granddaughter boiling the Onça, a jaguar (before the child naughtily eats him for dinner) (*Tales of Transformations 4-6*) and, unexpectedly, that folk tale of other sub-continental Indians, famously adapted by Rudyard Kipling, in 'How the Leopard got his Spots'.

The richness of Ana Maria Pacheco's imagery is matched only by that of her imagination. Jewelled colours with real gold leaf; figures curved as tightly as within an egg or a tondo; jaggedly bobbing drypoints like the paper cut-outs in Anne Stevenson's poem, 'Four and a Half Dancing Men'[2]; in accomplishing the transition from sketch or painting to drypoint or etching and thence to three-dimensional sculpture, Ana Maria Pacheco is herself a mistress of myriad metamorphoses.

Notes

1 *Folheto,* (lit. pamphlet) in north eastern Brazil, cheaply produced with woodcuts bound with string and hung out for sale on a 'washing line' *(cordel).* See, for example, *Brazilian Popular Prints,* edited by Mark Dinneen, published by Redstone Press, 1995; and *Lampião and his Bandits : Literature of the Cordel in Brazil,* by Augustus Young, published by Menard, 1994.

2 Anne Stevenson, 'Four and a Half Dancing Men' in *The Collected Poems 1955-1995,* published by Oxford Paperbacks, OUP, 1996

Ana Maria Pacheco's 'The Longest Journey'

George Szirtes

We do not need much for the Ship of Death. It is the longest journey we shall ever make and the last, but D. H. Lawrence knows that little cakes, some wine, a few small cooking pans and a change of clothes will suffice. In that wonderfully autumnal poem, ripeness is all:

> The apples falling like great drops of dew
> to bruise themselves an exit from themselves . . . [1]

and we ourselves find an exit from the fallen self. The self falls like apples. It is as natural as that. But the fall coming is, the poem tells us, an almost thunderous fall on the hardened earth and death smells like ashes, as Lawrence says,

> . . . the frightened soul
> finds itself shrinking, wincing from the cold
> that blows upon it through the orifices . . . [2]

Precisely so. That is why Pacheco's figures are so cold and shrunken about the shoulders, why their arms and legs are stiff and their necks so tensely thrusted or twisted in anticipation. Apples and bodies are equally bruised. Our souls, says Lawrence, are "oozing through the exit of the cruel bruise", the rhyme hidden but exact. The black flood rises and it is inevitable it should do so, but there comes a flush of yellow, a flush of rose,

> . . . and the body like a worn sea-shell
>   emerges strange and lovely.
> And the little ship wings home, faltering and lapsing
>   on the pink flood,
> and the frail soul steps out, into the house again . . . [3]

It is after all a "fragile ship of courage, the ark of faith", and the reason it moves us so is because its faith is in our courage and our humanity, which is not a ghost in some machine but of the same essence as nature itself. It has taste and texture, a comprehensive specificity, resonance (it sees a harmony between bodies, apples and drops of dew), and is capable of changing – astonishingly, miraculously – from the worse to the better.

In the meantime, of course, it has other predilections and preoccupations, predilections dealt with elsewhere in Pacheco's work.

The relationship between text and picture is complex. On the one hand we have illustrations, programmatic art, the whole apparatus of iconography and the signifier/signified model in all of which meaning is notionally transferred from one language to another. A picture is not itself a text of any kind though it may maintain intermittent contact with one and may, of course, produce a text in others. *The Longest Journey* as a set of carved figures in a real boat makes conscious reference to D. H. Lawrence's poem, 'The Ship of Death', but maintains contact only with the artist Pacheco's own

The Longest Journey, 1994

The Longest Journey, 1994

The Longest Journey, 1994, detail

The Longest Journey, 1994, detail

reading of the poem, a reading which naturally selects and develops. *The Longest Journey* resonates with 'The Ship of Death', and our association of the two works makes for a richer, more enjoyable reading, but the sculpture is not an interpretation of the poem as such. It brings a whole new hinterland to the perceptions discovered in the poem by the artist, a hinterland which includes Pacheco's own oeuvre to date, which in its turn encompasses interpretations of that oeuvre and other references comprehended by it. The task of an essay such as this is to describe, summarise and present its own reading which, with any luck, may supplement the pleasure and power of the work for the spectator. In the process it must ask: what kind of a thing is this? How does it move us? How does it matter?

So, what kind of a thing is it? Clearly, it is related to the tradition of Baroque religious sculpture in Brazil. It is a grouping of figures consciously referring to, and indeed employing part of the world beyond art. The boat is a real fishing boat, bought in Wroxham, dismantled for easy carriage then reassembled and strengthened to serve its new purpose. People outside the world of galleries have used the boat for its primary function. They have fished in it. Between 1796 and 1798 the extraordinary Brazilian artist known as O Aleijadinho ('The Little Cripple') produced a set of sixty-six carved figures in polychromed wood for the Sanctuary of Bom Jesus of Matosinhos at Congonhas do Campo, Brazil. Among these was *The Last Supper* group arranged around a circular table with a white cover. The table is a real table, the stools the apostles are sitting on look perfectly usable stools, the room in which the apostles are dining is the first of the six chapels of the *Stations of the Cross* but looks like a white room with corner cupboards. It is, after all, a room.

It might be useful to see this as a kind of theatre. That which is real in a dramatic production is real here. A table, some stools, a pair of corner cupboards on a stage are not acting: they are what they are. It is only the actors who are pretending to be someone else, employing the languages developed for them by the conventions of drama. We willingly suspend our disbelief. In O Aleijadinho's work, instead of actors we have expressive blocks of wood who, if we willingly suspend our disbelief, appear to be employing the language developed for them by the conventions of sculpture, which in turn depend, at least partly, on the conventions of theatre, which in turn . . . and so forth. The whole tendency of the Baroque, as it has been often noted, was to dissolve distinctions, to perform a kind of vulgar alchemy of the imagination. It sets out to confuse our senses so as to point us to realities beyond: of ecstasy, of martyrdom, of the impending presence of the world pressing through its material confines. This process parallels Lawrence's notion of the self leaving the self. Wölfflin long ago pointed to the nature of Baroque as flux.[4] It might explain why the empirical English mind, which refuted Berkeley by kicking a stone, has never really taken to it. Baroque posits existence as a kind of floating, the drama of the world as illusion, an illusion open to manipulation. This has its own eros. Didn't the naked girls at Wyndham's Theatre stand perfectly still in tableaux? The eroticism lay in the possibility of movement. The arrest wasn't final. It was only a little death after all.

The puritan Northern mind has never taken to Baroque. It rejected, and still does reject, both the rhetoric and the core apprehension on which it is based. Even the world of galleries which makes certain claims to speak an inclusive language subsuming Baroque finds it inimical. Galleries are rarely like theatres. In some ways they resemble the dedicated rooms of mansions and palaces from which they developed. Following the decline of organised religion they have grown rather more like the Dutch churches depicted by Pieter Saenredam in the seventeenth century – white, clear, high-minded sanctums for what is in fact quite a rigid orthodoxy. They refuse to pander to sensation. Like Saenredam's churches they are a historical phenomenon, as moving in their own way, and as transient. The attendant's chair is on no condition to be confused with an exhibit. The brick on the floor is not the brick on the building site. How dare you think of such a thing?

Just as O Aleijadinho's *The Last Supper* is properly situated in the chapel for which it was created, so Ana Maria Pacheco's *The Longest Journey* yearns for its appropriate theatre. The first time I saw it it was in the empty factory Pacheco was using as her studio. Immense, in half-light, and not yet fully assembled, the figures lay in various dark corners of the space, not yet gathered aboard. They were still being prepared for the journey, being cut or burnt or painted. One was aware of them as souls in the making. The heroic assembling of the boat for its exhibition in the Gas Hall, Birmingham, was almost as much part of the theatre of its being as the final splendid artefact. The souls were in position, the bow facing the exit doors. One almost wished the boat to move on out into the street and seek out the darker places of the soul whence it had come.

Work in progress, 1994

The Ship of Death moves on the longest journey. Its destination, according to Lawrence, is oblivion. It is autumn and the fruit is falling. On board there is a group of five robed figures in the bow, and immediately behind them, perhaps only vaguely associated with them, a set of five including two seated women, one of whom may be the daughter or younger sister of the other, and three male figures, one a child naked from the waist down, standing on a stool (a perfectly serviceable real stool), one dressed in a striped vest glancing apprehensively over the stern, and a third, a boy-man, naked from the waist up, straight backed, with severely cropped hair, looking at the sky. One could move among this group and find a space to sit down and get to know them as individuals, since their individuality is as important to the piece as their grouping. Take the robed figures at the front. They may well be angels or psychopomps. One is certainly female, one male, and the three others somewhere in between. One is wearing the skull cap often sported by Pacheco's figures, something like a silvered swimming cap, with a touch of the Etruscan or Egyptian about it. Amenhotep IV wears one in the state museum in Berlin. Here perhaps it is the cap of death or the helmet of invisibility. Regarded as a group, it is their robes and their separation that mark them out, but their faces wear perfectly human expressions. One with flying hair turns back to look over her shoulder, one leans over examining the state of the black flood below, a cropped haired figure examines the sky and the weather, the capped one looks sadly down, fearful or resigned. The one at the very front has drawn its cloak up to its mouth and glares ahead in a sinister fashion. I say sinister but I cannot be sure. The body language is ambivalent. In an earlier introductory essay to the works of Ana Maria Pacheco, Andrew Brighton once made the point that we are educated early into reading body language in fellow human beings but what we read may depend on who we are.[5] Body language may be dissimulated in any case. Actors do it all the time. But here, we are convinced, it is not a case of dissimulation. These bodies and faces are all we have: they can neither dissimulate or change. They are more compactly, more tellingly themselves than any human being or actor could be. This lumpen wooden sense of being has always been an important part of a statue's business. But if the statue is part of a group there is also the relationship between it and the other individuals, as well as its relationship to the group as a whole to consider. In this case, since there are five psychopomps and five human beings, we might imagine each psychopomp to be some sort of guardian

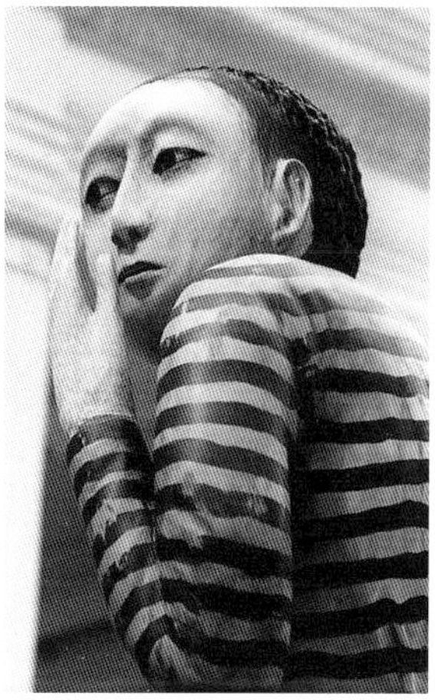

The Longest Journey, 1994, detail

The Longest Journey, 1994, detail

angel to one of the human beings. Of the latter, two are facing the front, the other three have their individual concerns, but there is a greater implied intimacy between them, if only because a sense of responsibility is inevitable when adults and children are together. There is certainly tenderness here, for even the adults have something childish about them. Their heads are large compared to their shoulders, their limbs move stiffly, their faces hide nothing. To ask whether these are good or bad adults or children, heroes or villains, whether they deserve the fate that is coming to them, is beside the point. They do not invite such questions. In converting them into text, I have inevitably turned them into something more prosaic, more narrative, more consecutive than they are. They are presences inviting us to enter their space – but only to a point. We cannot enter them without entering ourselves, without becoming more like them, as compact and truthful and ambivalent.

The Longest Journey, 1994, detail ▸

It may be useful to give some thought to these faces and bodies as mere physiognomies, because our relationship to them, their Baroque presence, is to some extent determined by their appearance. The typical Pacheco figure resists flow. The shoulders are slightly hunched, the torso stiff, the musculature, where indicated, is stumpy and simplified. They have dolls' bodies and, particularly, dolls' limbs. The arms are inflexible, tapering to wrists and tiny hands. The figures rarely rest firmly on the ground. Usually they are slightly tipped one way or another (a Baroque trait), implying incipient movement. The clothes they wear perform the role of drapery and are extremely expressive. I think immediately of Giotto's figures in the Arena Chapel, Padua, and suddenly everything seems a little clearer. The stiff bodies, the monumentality implied in that stiffness, is offset in Giotto by the dramatic handling of drapery. Think of the *Lamentation Over the Dead Christ*, the thunderous fall of drapery about the dead Christ's head, the controlled leaping and wailing of cloth as it falls and rises over his torso and feet. In Giotto, the faces being on the whole inexpressive, the clothes serve as the vehicles of feeling. The outside, the incidental, becomes an emblem of that inner essential state shared by figure and spectator. And all the more powerfully so because it is forced to work against the resistance of the face and body. Feeling is not simply thrown at us like something cheap of which there are yards to spare, but is conserved; feeling reserves itself to be read as involuntary truth, not rhetorical display. One might describe this notion of feeling as classicism in action, and in describing it so we become aware that Pacheco's work is not exclusively Baroque in origin. Look at the robes of the psychopomps, the skirts of the women and the rumpled vest of the little boy standing on the stool, then think of Giotto. There is power in such modesty. It doesn't billow or swirl but it is passionate, tender and pathetic. It speaks the language of music and association but the stiffness of the bodies resists it and lends it a kind of welcome curtness.

Then there are the heads, sitting on very short necks, with small craniums, low foreheads and tiny chins, a great breadth of cheekbone housing shallow glittering eyes, between which long thin noses descend over small vulnerable mouths full of little teeth. The impression is of something flat, like a drawing, everything a touch schematic. These are not the heads of intellectuals, yet their essential shape and proportion is not unlike those of the angels one finds staring down from the roofs of so many East Anglian churches. Their flatness resists elegance, their realistic eyes and teeth render them altogether more terrestrial, perhaps even slightly fetishistic. They are like children and adults remembered from childhood. Louis Simpson's marvellous poem 'My Father in the Night Commanding No' has just such characters.

The Longest Journey, 1994, detail

The Longest Journey, 1994, detail

. . . They will not change
There, on the stage of terror and of love.

The actors in that playhouse always sit
In fixed positions – father, mother, child
With painted eyes.
How sad it is to be a little puppet!

Their heads are wooden. And once you pretended
To understand them! Shake them as you will,
They cannot speak.
Do what you will, the comedy is ended . . . [6]

The Longest Journey, 1994, detail

The Longest Journey, 1994, detail

Pacheco's heads emerge out of the same world albeit at different angles. Even their clothes – if one looks at them carefully – refer to a form of yesterday. No wonder they are heading for oblivion.

The elements of these figures shift a little then come into occasional focus. Dramatic Baroque presence is combined with classical austerity and memories of a child's comprehension of adult seriousness, which, in the end, is not full comprehension, merely an apprehension that leaves and apples fall and time presses on.

The above represents an attempt to locate an answer to my first question: what kind of a thing is it? The answer to the second – how does it move us? – is to some degree implicit in that answer. It moves us through elegiac ripeness, communicating with us through the dramatic means of form, gesture, association, restraint, presence. It moves us because it strains and creaks at the limits imposed by gallery life while most contemporary art actively colludes with it and would be nothing, or much less, without it. It moves us also because it is unashamedly human and humanist in its assumptions. I am aware that the term 'humanist' may not be precise enough. Baroque is primarily a religious and religiose art. Modern European life provides ample examples of religiosity and shadow ritual (one only has to think of the ironic cult of celebrity and the often ironic pomp that goes with it) but very few of straight religion and ritual. Protestant gallery art is some sort of religion substitute with its own notions of the sacred. It is prone to precisely the same kind of corruption that tainted puritanism. On the one hand it tries to contain and place religiosity by placing itself on a moral and aesthetic pedestal; on the other it feeds off speculation, publicity and greed. For many of us it has been dead a long time and its formaldehysed corpse is stinking all over Europe. In Ian Starsmore's interview with the artist, Pacheco remembered her education in Goiás: "Then when you leave the building [the university] you go out to confront this landscape and ecology that has nothing to do with what you have learned . . . everything is thin, uncertain, distorted, scared and fearful like an animal hunted . . . "[7]

How does this matter? Pacheco's achievement is the recovery of that uncertainty in European terms. The religious and the religiose are part of the same experience and one is not ashamed of the other. The ritual is straight. The boat wants to sail out of the gallery into the tangible world. To do that is an act of courage and faith, which takes us back to Lawrence's fragile ship, and its destination which offers no false comforts, only something that might or might not be hope, which is hope without realising that it is.

Notes

1-3 D. H. Lawrence, 'The Ship of Death', from *Last Poems*, 1932.
4 Heinrich Wölfflin, *Principles of Art History*, First English Translation, 7th Edition, Dover Books, 1932.
5 Andrew Brighton, *The Work of Ana Maria Pacheco*, Pratt Contemporary Art, 1994.
6 Louis Simpson, 'My Father in the Night Commanding No' from *At the End of the Open Road*, Wesleyan University Press, 1963.
7 Ian Starsmore, 'Inventing the Black Powder' Art and Education', Pratt Contemporary Art, 1989.

The Longest Journey

Jane Farrington

The image of a boat in Pacheco's work first appears in two drypoints of 1987, *The Longest Journey I & II.* The figures squash claustrophobically and uneasily into the boat hull against the backdrop of a prominent mast and sail. Pacheco has used the medium of printmaking for experimentation and the working-out of ideas since her student days at the Slade in the early 1970s. This has often led to drawing and painting before finally attempting the inflexible medium of carving. Pacheco describes this process of discovering the image as a journey or, more accurately, a circumnavigation around the idea. It has parallels with Pacheco's first language, Portuguese, which avoids directness but always circles around a subject. More recently, the series of ten drypoints entitled *Terra Ignota* (published 1994) explore further the archetypal idea of the Ship of Souls journeying through life and beyond. *Terra Ignota 7* has a familiar 'inferno' composition of a descent or rescue from hell or the underworld. In *Terra Ignota 6*, a hooded figure bound to a ship's mast is visited in the darkness by benign winged creatures. Most recently, this image has been developed in the much larger drypoint *The Dark Night of the Soul* (1994) with its title taken from the writings of the medieval theologian St. John of the Cross.

The myth of the human soul journeying to unknown territory has profound resonances for all cultures. The early Christian Fathers likened the Church to a ship in which the faithful found safety and were borne to salvation and thus the nave of a Church derives from the Latin *navis* or ship. We are also familiar with, for example, the symbolism of boat-models found in Egyptian tombs and with Nordic burial ships. The Norse word for these burial ships was *Indr* meaning boat, coffin and cradle. The myths of the soul's journey through death and re-birth are symbolic of humanity's quest for self-realisation. Often a heroic figure becomes the people's agent or scapegoat who must face what they most fear during the 'dark night of the soul'. The hero is the archetype of the self, and, according to Jung, "the archetype of the self has, functionally, the significance of a ruler of the inner world, i.e., of the collective unconscious"[1] This process of self-realisation is about confronting the dark side of our own selves. In confronting, we begin to understand and therefore disarm evil of its power. In our modern post-Freudian times, the descent into Hell or Hades becomes the descent from consciousness into the unconscious. Pacheco, herself, cites Arnold Böcklin's *Island of the Dead* as a work that she admires for its treatment of the voyage to the underworld myth and the mood it creates. In Western culture, a figure robed in white is associated with death and the supernatural.

The central hero/scapegoat of *The Longest Journey* is the small half-naked boy standing on a stool. None of the images used in the prints, drawings and paintings leading up to the final sculpture prepare us for this vulnerable, sacrificial figure. The only visual link might be the small girl who appears in one of the *In Illo Tempore* paintings, and related prints and drawings. The strong Christian allusion in the male child is comparable to the leading figure in *Man and His Sheep* of 1989 and, most overtly, to the *St. John the Baptist* heads of 1992. Not all the figures in the boat acknowledge his presence but those that do are aware of his significance. The seated woman and the standing woman turning round at the prow appear to play the role of maternal protector/intercessor. The huddle of figures at the back of the boat contrast with the awesome circle of figures at the prow whose white twisting drapery gives them a transient, hallucinatory appearance.

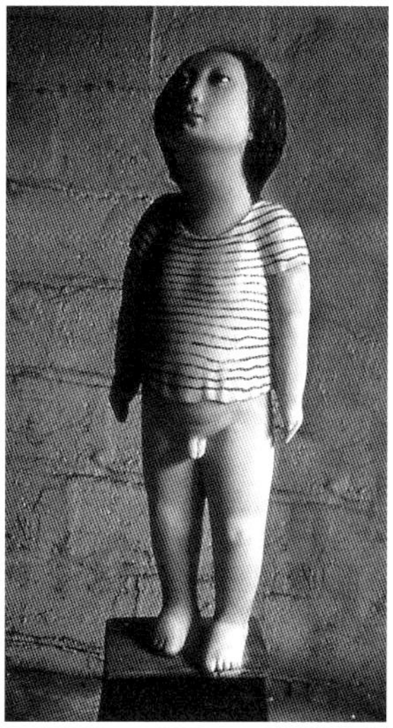

The Longest Journey, 1994 detail

In Illo Tempore I, 1994, detail

The turning point in the artist's early career was an experience of almost visionary intensity while she was a student at the Slade. Having made the initial 'leap in the dark' by her decision to leave Brazil for good to study at the Slade in 1970, she suffered a traumatic period of isolation and cultural dislocation reaching a point of desperation. Pacheco describes how she was in a darkened lecture room at the Slade and, at a moment of despair, suddenly and vividly recalled the Brazilian religious processions she had witnessed as a child. Taken by her aunt to these night-time street processions, she had witnessed the elaborate carved religious effigies with their glinting eyes, teeth and real hair carried aloft by candle-light. The rural region of Goiás where Pacheco spent her childhood was still culturally isolated and virtually unchanged since the nineteenth century. Pre-Christian and Christian rituals came together in these processions, and Pacheco remembers such haunting images as a small girl chosen to stand on a stool, covered in a black veil. It is no coincidence, therefore, that the little girl in the *In Illo Tempore* series also stands on a stool while a grotesque procession trundles behind her in the darkness. Pacheco understood that these memories of her earliest experiences in Latin America were to be her artistic motivation and inspiration and, at that moment, she commented, "the journey started".[2]

Now in her fifties, Pacheco is settled in England and is happy to remain in a country which gives her the freedom to live her own solitary and self-contained way of life. She is fascinated by the English characteristic of understatement and self-mockery. For Pacheco, as in her art, mockery sustains tension and drama.

A visit to Pacheco's studio is necessarily combined for me with a short journey to Norwich's medieval cathedral where the vivid and boisterous painted roof-bosses in the cloisters convey the same messages about ourselves that we see in Pacheco's art. In the midst of even the most fearful scenes, there is mockery and subversion and, therefore, hope and enlightenment. In our modern, 'hi-tech' and secular society, Pacheco reminds us, through her visual myth-making, that our vulnerability and mortality have not changed.

Notes

1 Carl Gustav Jung, 'Symbols of Transformation', p. 368, quoted in David Adams Leeming, *Mythology, The Voyage of the Hero*, 1981, p. 275.

2 The author in conversation with Ana Maria Pacheco, August 1994.

The Smile on the Face of the Tiger

David Elliott

The tragic limerick, the last line of which is quoted above, describes the demise of a feline-loving young woman who, in the short space of four lines, moves from riding on the back of a tiger to residing in its stomach. Like the Cheshire Cat she ends up as a smile. In this moral epic of foolhardiness, the smile is the sting in the tail and ostensible merriment conceals a cruel and heartless intent.

Ana Maria Pacheco has a similar taste for turning situations on their heads. Conventions are never quite what they seem and the light jab of playfulness which so characterises her touch moves us back against the ropes where, within a few seconds, the relentless pummelling of self-recognition leaves us gasping for breath. In other bouts, unimpeded by the false security of the viewer, jocular torturers compete with rubicund moppets as to who can make the cruellest uppercut of all. And then, during the wait for the referee to announce the victor, the terrifying complicity between victim and predator begins, slowly at first, to gnaw into our consciousness.

With time, just as people begin to resemble the animals which they keep in their household, the victim starts to adopt the mien and mannerisms of his oppressor. There are no consoling tableaux here of black vs white, right vs wrong, good vs bad – Pacheco's creatures all bear a family likeness both to the artist herself and to their unsuspecting audience.

A sense of drama runs throughout all of Pacheco's work; the characters seem like marionettes into whose actions human endeavour has been concentrated and crystallised. We are not contemplating a play or allegory with a firm moral, a beginning and an end, but a parallel to the confusion of battle.

As has been the case with many artists who have chosen the inevitability of human folly as their subject, Pacheco synthesises a contemporary mythology out of ancient sources. *In Illo Tempore* ('In That Time') is a chronicle of riddles, journeys, voyages, secrets, temptations, seductions and deaths; the figure of a woman or young girl runs decisively throughout them all – captivating and being held captive on a near life-sized scale. The size and composition of these paintings is important: gesso, sometimes gilded, on wooden panel suggests the opulence of the medieval icon in which the head of the saint or holy mother shines out of the surrounding darkness. But Pacheco does not use a traditional method of working, she has invented her own way of building up colour and shape with sponges and rags, rather than brushes, in laying down a succession of transparent washes to form a translucent space within each painting. The effect is like that of a series of spotlights which picks out the journey that envelops the viewer.

Some of the women that pass by seem familiar: Pornocrates – the woman with the pig; the Sphinx; Salome and Judith – the slaughterers; the woman on the swing – the seductress. They are all images of primordial female power – a force which transcends the vagaries of sexual dalliance to grasp the terrifying responsibilities of the act of creating.

Self-sufficiency and the invention of different ways of working are important to Pacheco. The bodies of her sculptures are charred with burners and hacked by chain-saws, their mouths are filled with individually made acrylic teeth. There are a few superficial similarities with Colonial sculpture of the sixteenth and seventeenth centuries which she would have known from the churches of her native Brazil, but such influences are not decisive. In her mind's eye, Pacheco uncovers the characters which populate her work by repeatedly using drawing as a rehearsal for the encounter which will culminate in the larger painting or sculpture. The pictorial, the graphic, the material and the sculptural, so often specialisms within the field of art, are for Pacheco part of a carefully balanced and mutually dependent continuum.

In her most recent work in wood, *The Longest Journey*, Pacheco has embarked on yet another voyage. The obsession with human scale has continued for the boat is real, yet it is difficult to tell from its occupants whether we should regard it as a Ship of Fools whose inhabitants progress blithely towards an end of their own engineering, or whether, more hopefully, this is a form of modern Ark where there is at least some likelihood of future salvation.

Pacheco's pessimism suggests the former, yet not all would be lost for a redemption of sorts may be found within the necessary struggle to realise each work. But if the boat is an Ark there is one possibility of which we may be sure: when the storms are spent and the flood waters subside, the first, and no doubt only, animal to leap to the land will be an overweight tiger with a radiant smile.

Untitled, Study for Painting, 1991 ▸

In Illo Tempore: ten paintings by Ana Maria Pacheco

Paul Hills

Once upon a time . . . *In Illo Tempore,* the title of Ana Maria Pacheco's paintings proposes a mythical time. The ten paintings belong to a set, not a sequence, and their numbering *I* to *X* is a labelling for convenience, not a mandatory order. Perhaps, like a cycle of fairy tales, there are several stories but each is the same story, and where we end is where we started from . . . Once upon a time.

The narratives of *In Illo Tempore* are open to the spectator to order and re-order. Just as in a fairy tale, repetitions and reversals wind up the spell, congruities and patterns in design build into a kind of visual incantation. The longer one contemplates the paintings, the more the apparently formal elements, such as striped pedestals, the axial presentation, or the curtains and cords, become integral to the subject, and what may have been invented by necessity of design turns into a magician's accessory. Consider, for instance, the striped pedestal on which a little girl and the young woman stand: observe how the paler stripes change from red to green, to red, to blue, and how the same blue stripes reappear on a cushion, its luxurious softness gently indented by the trotters of a wild boar; and then note how these blue stripes take to the air, hanging vertical as the blindfold suspended in front of the eyes of the Sphinx.

Before the creatures of the imagination can have a habitation, they need to find their mode of presentation, their frame. As a sculptor, Ana Maria Pacheco has explored the way in which the figure, and particularly the head, as a physical presence is both seen and itself sees. In a multifigure piece, such as *Man and His Sheep,* the spectator is drawn to approach the group and to intrude between the figures, and in doing so regards and is regarded. In her paintings Pacheco does not attempt to do what can be done better in sculpture, but rethinks the issue of staging. Several are divided or bounded by curtains or hangings, which reveal and conceal, both externally for the spectator and internally for the central protagonist, the girl or woman. They are theatrical. They evoke the constriction of Punch and Judy and its attendant violence; and they suggest an edge between make-believe and a world outside. Rather than being a safe demarcation, this edge is itself perilous and perhaps ironic, open to inversion. In *V* the juxtaposition of half-drawn curtain and laundry-basket, hitched as a chariot, ushers us into a world where bedclothes, dressing and undressing, are ravelled in a dream. To look on is to travel back to the primal anxieties of playing Peep-Bo, the game in which the infant dares to court absence and in so doing discovers the presence of self and other. And Pacheco's *mise-en-scène* calls to mind Melanie Klein's argument that adult fascination with curtains as ritualised in theatre has its roots in the infantile experience of bedclothes and mothers' skirts and petticoats. Like spectators at a play, before Pacheco's paintings we remain upon the threshold, sometimes teasingly kept at bay: the blindfold that hangs over the eyes of the Sphinx (*VIII*) is shared; it lies on the surface between two worlds, at once blindfolding the Sphinx and, by masking her eyes, partially cutting off the spectator as well.

Staging as pictorial device merges with staging as metaphor. The fate of woman, as bodied forth in these paintings, is to display herself. The central protagonist, whether set on a pedestal or suspended in air, is always female: and at the start, as a young girl, she appears as if isolated in the glare of footlights, surrounded by shadowy witnesses, and called upon to go on parade. Upon reaching womanhood, she is displayed before

In Illo Tempore IV, 1994

In Illo Tempore VIII, 1994

the people – *Ecce Femina* – a bikini for a loin cloth. Woman is tempted, judged, mocked, and yet through her display may gain a measure of power. Contraries are never far away: in the words of the Sphinx, *'Ego genero lumen sed tenebrae meae naturae sunt'* (I generate light but darkness is part of my nature).

In Illo Tempore VIII, 1994, detail ▸

Display relates to appearing, to process, to coming into being. Working on the figures of the women in *Man and His Sheep*, Pacheco burnt the wood to lend a degree of abstraction to their draperies, and when she quenched the fire the clouds of steam enveloping the figures set off a fertile train of imagery in her prints. Process suggests meanings; the search for the right process is itself a quest for meaning. Typically, Pacheco discovers her images, gives them free reign, and follows their transformation over a period of years. With each new medium comes a new inflexion: thus the imagery of *In Illo Tempore* depends upon themes uncovered in prints, big charcoal drawings, small paintings and pastels. The artist is humble before the craft of her medium; she allows it to prompt and to suggest; then from one medium to another something surprising is carried over. The communion of darkness and light proper to black and white media is transfigured in the paintings into a primordial brilliance of colour.

Coming into being is of the essence. The colours of *In Illo Tempore* glow like jewels, radiant from within. Pacheco uses pure oil colour, applied straight from the tube without mixing on a palette. At the start, in the process of what she terms 'coming to know', the marks on the panel are free, even gestural, but once an apt image begins to emerge, the artist brings it to realisation self-effacingly, deliberately losing the marks, expunging the trace of authorial intervention. Pacheco is categorical on this point: she distrusts any fetish of the brushstroke, the egoism of mark-making as signature. When, in 1993, she saw Giotto's frescoes in Padua she recognised what she was striving after: in fresco, so thin and smooth, no mannerism of the mark delays perception of the image or gets in the way of the narrative. Unlike the medieval artist, the contemporary one is denied a given or pre-ordained story, but Pacheco works towards an analogous transparency of medium – one that will allow the mind free passage to archetypal imagery.

After the initial stages of painting she renounces brushes, and uses cotton buds to deposit layers of colour. It is a technique she has developed in polychroming her sculptures. When the paintings are examined closely one discovers a lively freedom in the application and often a looseness of weave. The forms can breathe, emergent between darkness and light. Cumulatively the effect is a build-up of layers of transparent colour as though by a natural process of sedimentation. At the end the paintings are waxed rather than varnished, so that they are glowing rather than shiny. The finished paintings are radiant images that quite literally appear before our eyes – as if self-generated, powered from within.

A subject that recurs in manifold guises in prints, drawings, sculpture and paintings is decapitation. Pacheco remembers that when she was a child the Brazilian government caught a gang of notoriously violent bandits, known as 'Cangaceiros', decapitated them, and dispatched their heads around the country as a touring exhibition. A photograph in the newspaper of this admonitory spectacle left a deep impression on the young girl, and it was an image that came back to the artist many years later. Such a story reminds us that in Latin America the power of images was not purely aesthetic: objects were often put on show that were apotropaic (serving to frighten), or intended to bring about healing, or give thanks for healing, as with the votive objects placed in Catholic shrines.

After growing up in a society in which violence was not so much witnessed as sensed as a threat ever-present beyond the protection of the home, Ana Maria Pacheco would find nothing exaggerated in the violence of certain biblical narratives, or of Greek myths, and for a number of years her images have drawn on aspects of the stories of Judith and Holofernes, and Salome and John the Baptist, the most celebrated decapitations of men inflicted by women. Many artists have treated these stories in terms of conflict between male and female, sometimes interpreting a decapitation as a symbol of castration. In Pacheco's work it is not the opposition of the sexes, but the subtle exercise of power by an older woman over a younger one that is dramatised. Recently she remarked that the influence of mother over daughter is private while that of the father is essentially public, and that the private influence is the more compelling. At the Banquet of Herod, as related in St Mark's Gospel, it is Herodias who persuades her daughter Salome to dance before her step-father, King Herod. The older woman achieves her revenge on John the Baptist by exploiting the power of her daughter to please a man, for it is Herodias who tells Salome to ask the King for the head of the Baptist to be presented on a platter.

In the Old Testament story of Judith it is the young woman who is the model of virtue, but here too there is another woman, the maid, who as accomplice carries away the head of Holofernes in a sack. Characteristically, Pacheco conceives of the maid as an older, experienced woman.

At least four paintings of *In Illo Tempore* have resonances of the Judith/Salome stories. In *VII* an old woman, spectre-like in mask and cloak, makes a visitation to a bikini-clad girl. In *II* a young woman is offered a white sack by a pair of winged creatures, while another kneels before her in mock obeisance. In contrast to this demurely clad woman, the costumed virago of *III* triumphantly holds up a severed head. Like the armadillo in *VII*, the virago breathes fire, as though fully in command of consuming passion. In *IV* two women stand upon a wheeled platform and here, as in other paintings, threads or strings too fine to fulfil their literal function delineate psychic dependencies: one woman holds a bag suspended by pulleys at a slight distance; the other, vested in a coat of animal fur and bearing a ram's head, holds a thread attached to the float. Both turn to gaze at the igniting sack, and their two profiles, straight and long from brow to tip of nose, evidently belong to one family. The ram is aged, has foresuffered all, the head like a Mycenaean mask, vacant and golden.

In Illo Tempore V, 1994

Such imagery is powerful because it belongs to a world of archetypes, and any verbal paraphrase runs the danger of reducing it to illustration. Pacheco's finished paintings are effectively removed from identifiable narrative, thereby forestalling interpretative closure. Sometimes the archetypal resonance is achieved by conflation of myths. For a decade or more unidentifiable bags or packages have appeared in Pacheco's prints: the mysterious sack, which is the focus of attention in *II* and *IV*, may have begun life in drawings as the bag containing the head of Holofernes, and then in the process of working and reworking gathered something of the character of

In Illo Tempore VI, 1994

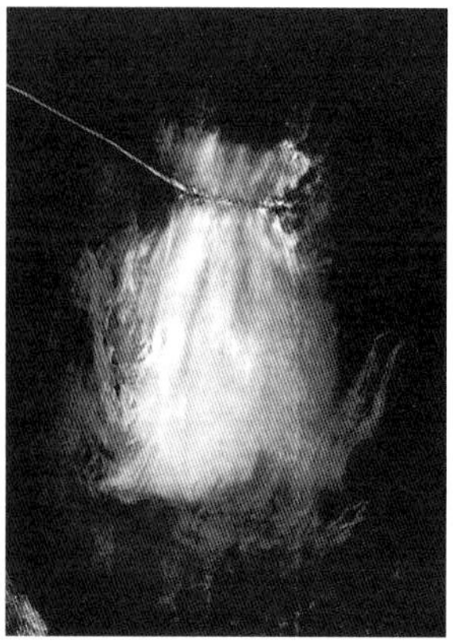

In Illo Tempore IV, 1994, detail

Pandora's box.

The myth of Pandora, famous from ancient Greek sources, is likely to have been mediated for Pacheco by the fiction of the great Brazilian novelist Machado de Assis. In Machado's masterpiece, known in English as *Epitaph of a Small Winner*, the narrator meets the primeval shape of woman and asks her what she is called:

> 'They call me Nature or Pandora. I am your mother and your enemy.'
> '. . . And why Pandora?'
> 'Because I carry in my bag all good things and all evils, and the most remarkable of all, hope, man's consolation. Are you trembling?'

When the narrator persists in wishing to live, in spite of the horrors natural to being alive, Nature/Pandora retorts:

> 'Why do you want to live longer? To continue to devour and be devoured? Are you not sated with the show and the struggle?' [1]

The bag in Pacheco's paintings may contain all good things and all evils, but it is in the scheme of things that neither we nor the artist are permitted to know for certain. What the passage from Machado de Assis reminds us is that Pacheco's imaginative world belongs to a vein of black humour, and to a tradition – stretching back to Cervantes' *Don Quixote* – of teasing the reader/spectator, shifting the boundaries of fiction (Machado's narrator is already dead), and of treating the world as a show in which pretence is crucial to the negotiation of life, spectres more real than flesh, and Folly a more powerful player than Reason.

In Illo Tempore VI, 1994, detail

As enigmatic as the bag or sack are the exhalations of fire and light. Again, luminous breath or *pneuma* has its genesis in Pacheco's prints: the wiping of ink upon the plate itself a breathing upon the waters, covering and uncovering. The drypoints, *The Dark Night of the Soul* and *Follies of a Guardian Angel*, and the screenprints, *Revelation*, rehearse the visitations of angels and fallen angels. Like Lucifer they are bearers of a light that entails darkness. Turning to the Apocalypse we read: "And I heard a great voice out of the temple saying to the seven angels, Go your ways and pour out the vials of the wrath of God upon the earth . . . And the fourth angel poured out his vial upon the sun; and power was given unto him to scorch men with fire." (Ch. 16, vs. 1, 8).

In *IX* of *In Illo Tempore* the woman holds a chalice or vial which is also perhaps a trumpet, a golden visor, a gasmask; like the evil or the knowledge that may escape from Pandora's bag, the exhalation is energy and anger. But the avenging angel, or the Fury from Greek drama (the creature hunched behind the pedestal in *III* might have escaped from a canvas by Francis Bacon) has another face. *Fiat lux*, light begotten not made, recalls *fiat mihi*: the girl on the trapeze (*VI*), her hands incarnadined, braves never-ending assumption.

In Illo Tempore IX, 1994, detail

Puppet on a string, or circus artist soaring on the high wire? Dependency or levitation? Hanging or apotheosis? Like exhalation, imagery of suspension, of trapeze or swing, recurs and with each recurrence grows more contrary. Consider the Sphinx. Her wings are not stretched for flight, but like a fur coat or feather boa they hang, at once drawn aside in erotic provocation and ready for embrace. A crimson cushion plumps out her love nest, its leaves in velvet pile. Alone of all the principals of these paintings, the Sphinx shows her teeth as well as her cupid-bow lips: she may kiss or wound, and her claws, extended like fingers, may caress or scar. No accident, then, that in the projection of design the nest takes on the conceptual delineation of a cage, endlessly swinging between earth and heaven.

"To continue to devour or be devoured." The words of Machado's Pandora foretell the imagery of rodent's teeth and the haunting of the human by the animal in Pacheco's paintings. At a superficial level one can point to biographical incident that might have served as trigger for some aspects of this bestiary, of these mythic encounters and metamorphoses. In Goiânia in the Brazilian state of Goiás, where Pacheco grew up, the boundary between the wild and the urban, the savage and the relatively civilised, was often transgressed: she remembers it was common to see wild pigs trotting fast through the city, and she heard stories of leopards attacking nearby farms. Aesop's *Fables* and Grimm's *Fairy Tales* were familiar reading. Many Brazilian fairy tales involved animals and were often extremely violent. Proverb and folklore were rich in animal metaphor. Tapir in Portuguese is *anta*, and Ana remembers that her father used to pronounce if a woman was very stubborn or coarse, "She is an *anta*". Parrots abounded and caged birds of all kinds (though not in the Pacheco household). Feather head-dresses were to be seen.

All these are fertile sources of conjunction between human and animal in folklore and in reality, but to understand Pacheco's use of animal imagery and what its import may be, we must look more closely at the paintings and mark where her figurative language distances itself from that of the Renaissance tradition and its heirs. In Greco-European thought vision is privileged as a nobler sense than touch, and the eyes are revered both as instrument serving the intellect and also as pathway to the soul. Hands, as servants of touch, feeding or labour, are inferior, but if used to gesture they are enrolled as instruments of language, visual signs of a faculty deemed to distinguish humans from animals. As a result, in the high narrative tradition of Western art there is, what one might call, a rhetorical alliance between soulful eyes and speaking hands. Pacheco, by contrast, reduces the size and articulation of hands so that they become more like paws and less capable of eloquent gesture. Similarly, the eyes of her figures no longer speak of the easy communication of the gaze, of a meeting of minds that transcends the body. Often the bone-whiteness of teeth thrust forward registers as starkly as the whites of the eyes, and whereas to read lips is to trace words or anticipate affection, to glimpse teeth is to arouse fears of carnivorous devouring.

By cutting the rhetorical alliance between eyes and hands (instead often bringing attenuated hands up to near the mouth), Pacheco's art shocks us into considering aspects of ourselves and how we relate to each other which the humanist tradition of representation has denied. Of course other artists in the twentieth century have done this, but few have done it with such achieved technique, such imaginative consistency, or such wit.

If the imagery of these paintings reminds us of the demons that are with us and within us, the monsters we must manage, the fact of their creation – the coming into being of these glowing images from a mythical time – is a kind of quietus, a discharge of debts, a sign of hope. We all need such wonder.

In Illo Tempore III, 1994

In Illo Tempore III, 1994, detail

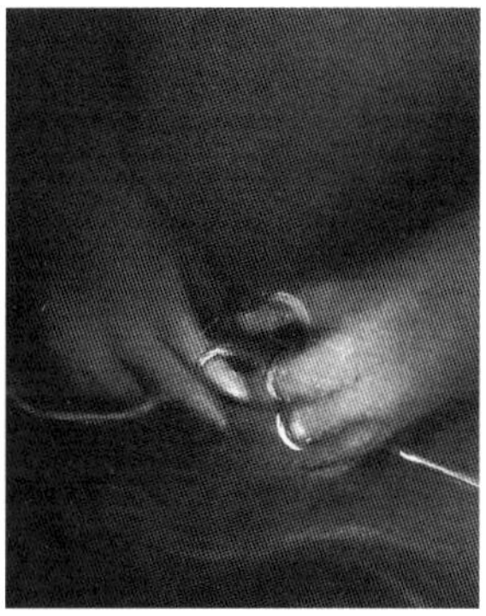

In Illo Tempore X, 1994, detail

Notes

1 From chapter 7, pp 18-19, translated by W. L. Grossman, London, 1953.

Ana Maria Pacheco – in context

Vivian Schelling

To write on the relationship between Ana Maria Pacheco's work and the culture of her native Brazil is a complex task. Works of art and literature, as sociologists of culture have pointed out, are not mere reflections of the social context in which they emerge. Consisting of invented forms, situations and characters and of many layers of meaning, they convey an imaginary vision of reality. As such they transcend the immediate social context in which they are nonetheless rooted and which provides the material and language through which the work is articulated. In attempting to trace the connection between a work of art and the culture from which it has sprung, it is necessary to avoid reducing it to an illustration of the culture. The relationship, particularly in non-illustrative or documentary forms of art is highly mediated. In approaching Ana Maria Pacheco's work I will thus discuss specific themes, dilemmas and traditions relating to Brazil and Latin America, which informing her vision find expression in aesthetic form.

Perhaps one of the most significant formative influences on Pacheco's work can be traced to her place of birth, Goiânia in the state of Goiás. Goiânia lies in the vast and desolate hinterland of central Brazil which until recently has remained isolated from the major transformations which have formed modern Brazil since the early twentieth century. Rapid industrialisation, the explosive growth of cities, the rise of a powerful labour movement, modernism and experimentalism in art and architecture, the development of radio and television have been concentrated in the South and coastal regions. This disparity between different regions, between a modern and pre-modern way of life, is rooted in the colonial inheritance and is of central importance in understanding Brazilian and Latin American culture.

European culture, transplanted to Brazil in the sixteenth century, established itself as the dominant and official high culture, while the native Amerindian and African cultures, brought to Brazil through the slave trade, became part of a marginalised non-official popular culture. Subsequently, in the nineteenth century, as Latin Americans sought to create modern republics following the struggles for Independence, France and England replaced Spain and Portugal as models to be emulated. Pre-industrial and pre-Enlightenment Iberian culture suffered a similar process of devaluation and marginalisation. Anguished by the thought of being constituted of marginal and 'backward' cultures, post-Independence intellectual elites attempted to reproduce European aesthetic and literary currents on Brazilian soil. Classicism, romanticism, realism, symbolism were transplanted to Brazil frequently with little adaptation to the local context, giving rise to a prevalent sense of discrepancy between the language and techniques of intellectual and aesthetic expression and local reality, between form and content.

This incongruity is overlaid by a further set of disparities arising out of the highly uneven process of economic development of different regions, a characteristic that is also a product of Brazil's colonial legacy. In response to European demand for raw materials, different regions flourished alternately, only to subside again into poverty and oblivion when market demand slackened. Journeying from the North and the hinterland in which the past still exists as an active force to the South, where the speed of social change and the production of wealth is most marked, is also a voyage through time in which the social relations and cultural forms of different epochs intermingle in discordant simultaneity.

◂ *The Dark Night of the Soul*, 1993-4, detail

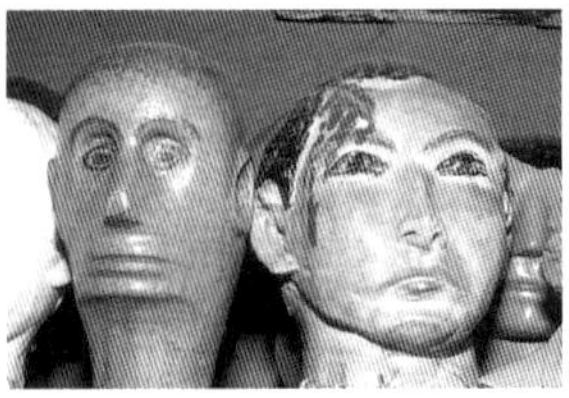

The Miracle House (1)

These incongruities and disparities have, one could argue, generated a sensibility to paradox, ambiguity and duplicity as well as a prevalent sense, often expressed in a form of black humour, that the manifest forms of social and cultural life conceal another reality, not fully acknowledged but all the more real. Beneath official Christian doctrine derived from the Vatican lies a mystical and messianic Catholicism, Amerindian myth and African polytheism with its emphasis on the body as the vehicle of divine energy. The appearance of representative democracy and its institutions conceals the arbitrary and despotic power of the landowning class, the State and the armed forces.

In the city of Goiânia, these incongruities were most certainly also part of the fabric of everyday life. While superficially acquiring the characteristics of a modern city, particularly since the construction of the capital, Brasília, not far away, Goiás remained essentially anchored in a pre-modern way of life. This rural and archaic world was characterised by the presence of two elements that infused existence with a frightening atmosphere of violence and mystery: large landed estates, the semi-feudal relationship between an oppressed peasantry and the all-powerful clans of landowning families and the Catholic Church. Due to the isolation of the region, the Catholicism which prevailed harked back strongly both to the Baroque and the Middle Ages.

The Devil, Woodcut (2)

In contrast to the modern optimistic belief in the perfectibility of humankind through reason, in the medieval conception humanity was in perennial danger of perdition through sin and folly, closer to beasts than angels. The quest for salvation was expressed through the extraordinarily rich panoply of rituals and imagery, involving religious processions, pilgrimages, penances and lively dramatisations of the life of Christ, the Prophets and the Saints, their revelations, martyrdoms and temptations. These dramatisations were originally introduced in the early colonial period by Franciscan and Dominican friars in the form of morality plays with the purpose of converting the indigenous population to Christianity. The Festival of St. John the Baptist, for example, represented to the population the sacrament of baptism, while The Nativity of St. John the Baptist explained the theological history of humankind until the redemption of humanity by the coming of Christ. In order to facilitate the process of conversion, native pagan dances and masquerades were incorporated into Catholic practices on holy days, while the states of suffering and ecstasy of the protagonists were rendered in vivid detail in order to inspire faith and terror.

This form of Catholicism contains in its more popular version a strong magical and pagan element. This is expressed not only in the very concrete belief in the existence of Satan and other supernatural beings, but in the conviction that the divine is effectively present and not merely represented in the statues and icons of the Christian faith. This blurring of boundaries between the real and the imaginary, the belief in the existence of an invisible world beyond the visible, renders ordinary reality extraordinary and a place in which miracles can occur.

Study of Head, John the Baptist III, 1992, detail

Pilgrimages in homage to a saint, virgin or religious prophetic figure in Brazilian history entails bringing votive offerings as an expression of gratitude for an illness healed or a problem solved. Most of the offerings represent the part of the body that has been healed through divine intervention. Heads, legs, arms carved in wood or moulded in clay or plaster by local craftspeople are brought to a special room in the church, called The Miracle House,[1] where they are kept. Other objects offered to the saint relate to specific lived situations in the life of the pilgrim, and they include photographs, baptismal and bridal gowns, candles, crosses, crutches, wheelchairs, strands of hair, a hoe, a radio. The heads however are perhaps the most expressive;

sometimes their form is simple and almost abstract, alternatively they are very realistic with eyes and mouth painted in great detail. Frequently the expression seems frozen in a state of grace.

Aleijadinho, *The Last Supper* (3)

In seventeenth century Brazil, the refinement of Church decorations grew, giving rise to an indigenous Baroque style, which in its unfettered imagination, extravagance, dynamism and theatricality has frequently been seen as the aesthetic form most attuned to the Ibero-American conception and experience of the world.

In Brazil, the high point of this American Baroque is manifested in the sculptures of Antônio Francisco Lisboa, known as O Aleijadinho, or 'The Little Cripple', due to the deformities which his body suffered as a result of several diseases. One of his most striking works is the Church of Bom Jesus of Matosinhos at Congonhas in the State of Minas Gerais. A steep road leads to the Church along which six small chapels with the Stations of the Cross have been erected. Christ's Last Supper,[3] Betrayal and Crucifixion are rendered with breathtaking pathos through the expressionistic and bold over-emphasis of certain features: the soldier's heads are oversized, their grotesque faces mirroring the ugliness of their emotions; Christ's face is sublimely beautiful and transfigured by his spiritual trial; tears are deeply carved into the stricken faces of the women who accompany him to the cross. On the balustrades of the staircase leading to the Church stand the prophets, among them Isaiah, Jonah, Ezekiel [4] and Jeremiah, their prophecies engraved in Latin on stone tablets. The chiselled figures of the prophets are positioned so as to give the viewer the impression of a complex choreographic pattern, their faces framed by flowing locks of hair and beard, transfixed by their prophetic vision.

Aleijadinho, *The Prophet, Ezekiel* detail (4)

Many of the themes and elements of form in Pacheco's work, as well as the general aura of her sculptures, etchings and paintings seem informed by the structure and feeling of this world. This can be seen in several aspects of her work: in the shape of her heads, in the non-naturalistic realism of her sculpture and rounded, sculpted quality of her figures recalling both popular and Baroque wood carvings; in the extraordinarily intense sense of the sacred in its terrifying and sublime aspects. The 'realness' of the eyes and mouth equipped with real teeth blurs the distinction between representation and reality in a visionary, hallucinatory way. In particular, in the head of *John the Baptist III* on a platter, in his sensual semi-open mouth, in its redness, somewhere between a kiss and a wound, the literal and untamed conception of the religious experience to be found in popular art is elaborated.

In a broader sense, the precarious condition of the human soul in this life caught in the conflict between the forces of light and dark, the daemonic and the sacred, is central to her work, frequently conveyed with the chiaroscuro and pathos of Baroque imagery. Humans struggle against irresistible forces pulling them into a dark underworld of annihilation. A seafarer stranded in a small boat and tied to a mast is visited by an Angel, a messenger of the divine, whose torch illuminates his darkness, *Terra Ignota 6.* The numinous light which he sheds on the imprisoned figure evokes a promise that he will be delivered from his solitude and blindness. In another drypoint of the same series, *Terra Ignota 3,* a little girl arrives on shore, on the same small boat. She is led by an older woman whose candle gives off a shining white light. In both images, it seems a truth unbearable to behold is at stake. The seafarer cannot see or act on what he sees, while the little girl raises her hand in astonishment at what the strange mystical light reveals. This theme is repeated in *Untitled Study for Painting*: a figure is imprisoned in a glass box and blindfolded by a striped cloth; above the figure an inscription in Latin states: 'I generate light but darkness is part of my nature'.

Terra Ignota 3, 1993-4

The perilous and ambiguous nature of human existence is graphically conveyed by the presence of figures who span different worlds, who are human and beast at the same time. Animals in the Christian world have frequently been used, as in the work of Bosch, to symbolise the 'lower' animal appetites and sensations; in Mayan culture every person has an animal alter ego or *nahuatl* which embodies the essential qualities of the person; in fables, animals are used to represent human virtues and vices, and in Brazilian oral literature humans are metamorphosed into animals as a consequence of moral transgression. The sense of equivocalness is heightened by the fact that the animal face in Ana Maria Pacheco's work is a mask concealing the identifying and humanising features of the figure. In *Follies of a Guardian Angel*, the juxtaposition of worlds is even greater in that here it is the divine and the bestial that meet: several 'fallen' angels, sporting animal masks, seem to delight in their fall and in the freedom it gives them to indulge in mischief, madness and deceptive play, for which no doubt in the 'high' world of Heaven, purged of the daemonic, there is no place. In these drypoints, the interrelation of opposites is playful and whimsical; ambiguity here refers to the subversive pleasure which being 'other' to one's official self provides.

Follies of a Guardian Angel 1, 1993

The mask is also emblematic of popular carnivalesque festivities in which the sense of contradiction between an apparent world of order and an underlying reality of chaos finds expression. During Carnival the norms which govern everyday life are temporarily relaxed, allowing feared and unspeakable truths to surface while social taboos are desecrated through satire and parody. Death, devils, fools, criminals and prostitutes, figures who destabilise the social order are enthroned. Carnival is a ritualistic theatre in which the 'lower' sphere of the body and its suppressed impulses displace the 'higher' sphere of order and moral decorum; aesthetically this is expressed in the grotesque, ironic and expressionistic distortion of form.

Follies of a Guardian Angel 4, 1993

One image in which grotesque distortion and parody appears clearly is in a drawing study for *The Banquet.* The experience of an unthinkable fear of annihilation is conveyed in the image of a naked figure lying prostrate before a group of bald, black suited men, who seem to wield absolute power over the fragile, defenceless victim which they are about to devour and possibly hang like a carcass by his feet for their delectation, as in *Acrobats.* Such representations hark back to a society in which those who rule respond to challenges to the legitimacy of their power with the brutality of the first Conquistadors and slave-owning landowners and miners towards Indians, Africans, peasants and servants. Since Independence in the nineteenth century, dictatorships have cast a long shadow over political life in Latin America, while the figure of the dictator has been the subject of several works of Latin American fiction. His arbitrary power is described with satyrical and carnivalesque exaggeration in García Márquez's *The Autumn of the Patriarch.* The patriarch is a dictator, who lives over 100 years; his tyranny is infinite and eternal and can only be described through the use of hyperbole:

"Previously, during the occupation by the marines, he would shut himself up in his office to decide the destiny of the nation with . . . his thumbprint, for in those days he did not know how to read or write . . . [he] governed orally and physically, present at every moment and everywhere with a flinty parsimony but also with a diligence inconceivable at his age, besieged by mobs of lepers, blind people and cripples who begged for the salt of health from his hands . . . and dauntless adulators who proclaimed him the corrector of earthquakes, eclipses, leap years and other errors of God . . ." [5]

The Banquet, study for sculpture, 1983, detail

The devouring homunculi in Ana Maria Pacheco's work are however less ridiculous and buffoon-like than Márquez's patriarch. Their technocratic anonymity speaks of a naked, robotic power to destroy which only modern states have marshaled against their populations. There is however also an element of humour and irony. *Acrobats* are dressed in striped 'canvas' bikinis, referring to the carefree and playful life of the beach and circus. This makes the images complex and dynamic in that the extreme seriousness of the subject matter is shot through with an irreverent gesture, making it difficult to rest in a morally one-dimensional attitude to the inhumanity depicted.

In *The Banquet* the figures have been equipped with a set of real teeth which are sharp and jut out from under the lips in a bestial manner. This virtual coming to life of the figure blurs the boundaries between art and life and renders the vision of human relationships as a mutual devouring particularly disturbing. Cannibalism as a metaphor for human relationships is a central theme in Brazilian cultural history. It was originally developed in the 'Cannibalist Manifesto' in the 1920s by the Modernist poet Oswald de Andrade. Using the image of the 'cannibalist' Indian as a metaphor for the relationship between the coloniser and the colonised, it proposed that Brazil overcame its perennial cultural dependence on Europe by selectively 'devouring' what Europe had to offer but in the process adapting it to local conditions. In the seminal novel *Macunaíma*, written in 1926 by Mario de Andrade, the hero, an Amerindian trickster figure journeys from his native Amazonia to the city of São Paulo to recover his lost amulet which has magically ended up in the hands of an industrialist who is also a fierce cannibalist giant intent on devouring the hero.

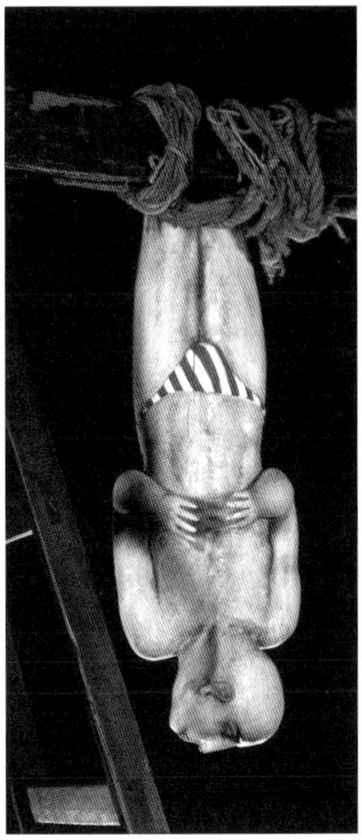

Acrobats, 1983, detail

This sacrilegious and disturbing view of human relations as a mutual devouring is perhaps particularly acute in societies where hunger is still an ever-present reality and where individuals are literally consumed in their battle to survive in a context of chronic economic insecurity and political oppression, impotence and unpredictability. Society appears to those who are subject to such circumstances as a devouring monster.

In many of Ana Maria Pacheco's images, one encounters a clustered group of people, either sitting claustrophobically together in a boat or frequently witnessing performances and terrible acts carried out by individuals. This conjures up notions of 'the crowd', 'the people' enthralled by the power of a charismatic individual. In the drawing *Beheaded (Judith)* the crowd sniggers and gasps as she triumphantly holds Holofernes' severed head in a bag; her charisma derives from the fact that she, a woman, has challenged male authority through a violent act of transgression. In the drypoint *Man and His Sheep I*, the Man carrying a sacrificial ram's head enthrals the crowd with his power. Like a circus acrobat, wearing only a striped loin cloth, his seductive power is represented by the reins connecting him and the crowd which he manipulates artfully in his performer's gloved hands. That his power emanates from the duplicitous and deceptive use of a mask seems to be conveyed in *Man and His Sheep II*, where, divested of the ram's head, he can be seen secretively chuckling to himself. Yet here too there is an element of ambiguity in that the archaic sacrificial quality of the ram's head seems to indicate that the relationship between himself and the crowd will be inverted and the leader himself will be sacrificed. These images recall paintings of Christ's Passion and the throng of base and ignorant people who flock to watch his humiliation and pain; they recall medieval paintings of market and feast days where ignorant and illiterate peasants delight in the spectacle of floggings and humans in stocks; they are reminiscent of scenes from the French Revolution and the pleasure and thrill derived from witnessing executions at the guillotine.

As an image of society or 'the people' and its relationship to power, these works could not be more distant from an optimistic representation of the collective. Portrayed as gullible, voyeuristic and ignorant, these images allude to the irrational and authoritarian political culture of Latin America, referred to as *caudilhismo*, based

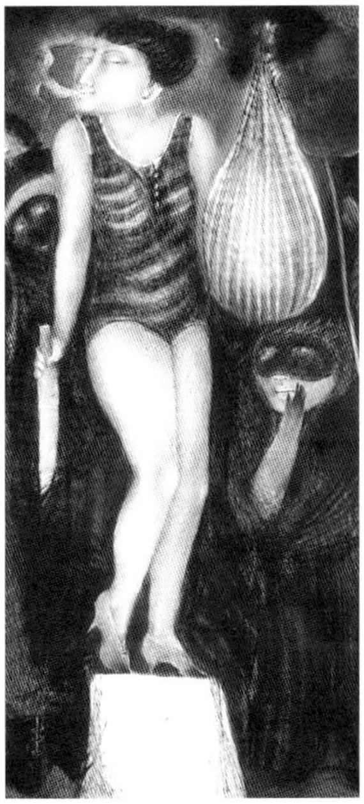

Beheaded (Judith), 1991, detail

on the duplicitous manipulation of the poor, illiterate and oppressed masses by charismatic leaders. However, these images are too allusive and archetypal to be seen only in such a specific historical context; they communicate in a broader sense a dark and critical vision of human desire and motivation. Yet they are not nihilistic; rather, their negativity is a forceful challenge to the viewer to acknowledge the full complexity and depth of human relationships; for though we may avowedly strive towards light, reason and civilised behaviour, the daemonic life of the passions has irresistible attraction. And it is perhaps from the standpoint of a third world country, marked by incongruities, disparities and multiplicity, on the margins of Western civilisation, that this uncomfortable perception of social life as a dangerous, darkly comical game of charade in which a secret – and often open – barbarism is at play, can be so richly elaborated.

Notes

1 The Miracle House (Sala dos Milagres), Trinidade, Brazil.
2 The Devil, woodcut, anonymous; North East Brazil.
3 Aleijadinho's *The Last Supper*, 1796-9; one of the Stations of the Cross at the Church of Bom Jesus of Matosinhos at Congonhas do Campo, Minas Gerais, Brazil.
4 Aleijadinho's *The Prophet, Ezekiel*, 1800-5, (detail); Church of Bom Jesus do Matosinhos, Congonhas do Campo, Minas Gerais, Brazil.
5 Gabriel García Márquez, extract from *The Autumn of the Patriarch*, Picador, published by Pan Books, 1978, p.10.

Circumnavigation: the poetics of exploration in the work of Ana Maria Pacheco

Simon Willmoth

It is now over twenty years since Ana Maria Pacheco came to England from Brazil to study at the Slade School of Art on a British Council scholarship. In her fiftieth year she has completed fifty new images in a range of print media. This essay will concentrate on the themes of these prints, their congruity with Pacheco's painting and sculpture, and on the role of printmaking in her art practice.

It is characteristic that the fifty new prints in this catalogue do not only use the intaglio methods with which she is familiar but also employ the techniques of lithography, screenprint and woodcut. By using a wide variety of techniques and mediums to create images, Pacheco maintains the challenge of the unknown which is vital to the sense of exploration in her work. In this way she is able to concentrate upon what she doesn't know about the image and to remain open to its possibilities. To further this, within the discipline of a particular print medium, conventional technique may be abandoned in order to develop an appropriate visual language. For example, the two huge woodcuts, *And They Inherited the Earth I & II*, were created by adapting the direct carving technique used in her sculpture, whereas the other two series of woodcuts, *Gargantua and Pantagruel* and *Five Imaginary Beings*, are on a much smaller scale and so required developing an entirely different technique, using the tools normally associated with the medium.

Confronting the problems and realising the potential presented by different printmaking mediums helps to avoid over-familiarity with the image, while enabling Pacheco to become intimately acquainted with it and with the ongoing themes of her work. This process of 'coming to know', through conceptual and formal experimentation in printmaking, crucially informs the production of Ana Maria Pacheco's sculpture without being simply preliminary to it. Such a process has been identified by Hélène Cixous as one of the insights she has drawn from the work of the Ukrainian-born Brazilian writer, Clarice Lispector:

"One of the first lessons about living is the one that consists of *knowing how not to know*, which does not mean not knowing, but knowing how not to know, knowing how to avoid getting closed in by knowledge, knowing more and less than what one knows, knowing how not to understand, while never being on the side of ignorance. It is not a question of not having understood anything, but of not letting oneself get locked into comprehension. Each time that we come to know something, in reality it is a step. Then we have to strike out for the un-known to make our way along in the dark, with an 'apple in our hand' like a candle." [1]

Gargantua and Pantagruel I, 1993-4

Pacheco describes the process of coming to the image as a journey, a circumnavigation. But this is not a closed journey through charted terrain, it is a journey into 'undiscover'd country': terra incognita; in Portuguese, *terra ignota.*

This metaphor of the journey or voyage does not only relate to the process of making Pacheco's work; it is also a recurrent theme of the work, and one which is particularly important in the present series of prints and for the next major piece of sculpture. The subject is not a new one in her work, though, appearing at least as far back as 1977 in the etchings *Between Mitcham and Croydon: the Heritage of the Aged.* This series drew on the prosaic experience of a regular bus journey to record the unknown figures as archaic landmarks. People have a physical presence and yet can also be fantastical, chimerical: these two spheres may be linked by memory and imagination.

Gargantua and Pantagruel VIII, 1993-4

The Longest Journey I, 1987

The Longest Journey II, 1987

And They Inherited the Earth I, 1993-4

An important motif within the theme of the journey is that of the ship or boat, which first appears in two large drypoints of 1987, *The Longest Journey I & II*, and recurs in *Perils of faith 2*, 1990 and in the series of ten drypoints completed in 1993, *Terra Ignota*. The longest journey is that of death, the voyage of oblivion, Hamlet's 'undiscover'd country'. The ship is the vessel that conveys the soul to its unknown destination, it is a motif that resonates many narratives and symbols in mythological and Christian iconography: the barque of Charon, the boatman who ferried the souls of the dead across the river Styx to Hades; the Ark; the Navicella, bearing the disciples, symbol of the Church – the vessel in which the faithful are safe and borne to salvation; the embodiment of the Navicella in the roof of the nave of each church; the Provencal legend of Mary Magdalene, adrift in a boat without sails, oars or rudder, being guided by an angel to land safely at Marseilles.

However, in Pacheco's Ship of Souls the focus is always located in the drama and vagaries of human behaviour, sometimes signified by the masks and animal heads. The petty alliances and betrayals of the playground and the boardroom are re-enacted; the flattery, posturing and jostling for position that we witness or engage in. In *The Longest Journey I* four figures are crowded together, and yet relations of power are evident in the looks they exchange, in the treachery or temptation being whispered; who has the ear of, who holds the candle and who the bound fish: "we shall be fishers of men". Similarly, in *Terra Ignota 2*, three figures nestle in the precariously suspended hull and cajole the petrified woman to step into the void, something these kings of infinite space would not contemplate for themselves: "soft language issued from their spittleless lips".[2] The black sail in *The Longest Journey II* acts as a backdrop to the drama, which consists of a male contemplating his next grandiose statement, while the female glances at us as if to acknowledge his pomposity; yet she remains wary of our gaze. The black sail recalls the triumph/tragedy of Theseus' return to Athens. After his journey to the Minotaur and through the Labyrinth, Theseus forgot to hoist white sails, the pre-arranged sign of success. His father, king of Athens, therefore read the black sails as signifying his son's death and in grief threw himself into the sea. Whereupon, triumph following tragedy following triumph, Theseus became king of Athens.

Therefore, although these are journeys into the unknown, into the imagination, and they explore the uncertainty of knowing, the territory of human interaction is all too familiar.

In the *Terra Ignota* drypoints the ships are fixed, in dry dock, perched on stilts like some ungainly animal, bolted to scaffolding above an ungainly animal – the leaden Rhinoceros – or hung from hooks like a swing. These cockleshells are not moving through space, just as the series does not form a linear narrative, nor do they chart a progressive course; there are no landmarks to show us where we are going, or if we are going anywhere.

In this manichean universe even the distinction between light and darkness is ambiguous: *Ego genero lumen sed tenebrae meae naturae sunt* (I generate light but darkness is part of my nature).[3] Of course in monochrome prints this distinction is vital as it determines the image. In Pacheco's prints this dualism reflects the difficulty of 'seeing the light', of having no light to guide, or of sheltering the candle, the symbol of both the light of faith and of the transience of human life. The candlelight of *And They Inherited the Earth I* seems to be absorbed into the darkness of the torturer, recalling Joyce's "ghostcandle to light her agony". The corrosive irony of the print's title only serves to further challenge the faith that one light might suffice in the dark. Here the woman is blindfolded, bound and suspended in a parody of angelic or acrobatic flight.

We might be tempted to observe, with Goya, "There is no one to save them".[4]

The seven etchings, *Quietus est*, also chart a journey of death and betrayal, with the light almost extinguished in plates 3 and 4 of the series: "darkness at one with darkness, up and down and sideways utterly dark so there is no direction any more".[5] However, the final image, *Quietus est 7*, suggests the possibility of redemption, albeit one which carries its own burdens, with its accompanying text from Isaiah: "Arise, shine for your light has come".

Terra Ignota 6, 1993-4

In *Terra Ignota 6* an angel breathes light on a bound and hooded mariner, a subject which is developed in the large drypoint *The Dark Night of the Soul*, in which the figure is more explicitly linked to the *Acrobats*. Here the angel's light or vapour soothes the mariner with its balm, yet its sensuality also torments him as he strains forward on tiptoe, an encounter which is rapturously witnessed by another angel. In both prints the vapour defines his form while remaining formless itself. The dark night of St. John of the Cross, which the title quotes, is a metaphor of the journey toward divine union, which he expresses in his poems and commentaries, *The Ascent of Mount Carmel*, and *Dark Night of the Soul*. The dark night of St. John's mystical experience does not reflect the absence of light but rather the overloading of human sensory and intellectual faculties by the pure light of the divine:

> Oh, night more lovely than the dawn,
> Oh, night that joined Beloved with the lover. [6]

This spiritual journey of transformation is not simply from the darkness into light, however. Pacheco's work suggests that journeys of the spirit are not necessarily spiritual journeys, and that the voyage might take a path from darkness through light to return to darkness. In the six lithographs *Don Quijote y Dulcinea*, a journey of union and separation is enacted, one which moves from imagination through desire and courtship by the mock-heroic suitor on a child's hobbyhorse, into the light of requited love; the lover transformed in the beloved. However, the darkness of jealousy and possession emerges as Don Quijote rejects and glowers at his faithful squire, Sancho Panza. In the final image he is isolated again, sitting in the gloom, hugging his loneliness.

Don Quijote 3, 1993-4

The congruence of the spiritual and the sensual, evident in the poetry of St. John of the Cross and in the 'Song of Solomon', is signified by the blown vapour, the mist that pervades Don Quijote's dream and that excites his desire; that draws travellers to the unseen shore in *Perils of faith 2*. This emanation is a potent draught and one that leaves many different traces: it is Circe's potion, it is the red miasma that flows like the blood of sacrifice and salvation from the first trumpet of the Apocalypse and settles like radioactive dust on the sinners below, in the screenprint *Revelation II*. The angels' blown light in *Terra Ignota 6* and *The Dark Night of the Soul* is also the Sirens' song: *mulier cantat*. Odysseus, the archetypal voyager, commands that he be bound against the song of the Sirens and that his bonds must be tightened should he struggle or gesture to his men to set him free. He thus experiences the promise of the Sirens' song without succumbing to its temptation.

Don Quijote 4, 1993-4

Adorno and Horkheimer have interpreted this episode of the *Odyssey* as an allegory not only of social class but also of the separation between manual labour and the enjoyment of art in Western culture. Odysseus is literally tied into his social role as the master, while the oarsmen do the work; they row past the Sirens, with their ears stuffed with wax. As a result the power of the Sirens' song is neutralised, the oarsmen cannot hear it and Odysseus cannot join with it, only contemplate the song as, "an inactive

Don Quijote 6, 1993-4

The Face of the Hero, 1976

This time they came to stay, 1978

eavesdropper like later concertgoers . . . So long as art declines to pass as cognition and is thus separated from practice, social practice tolerates it as it tolerates pleasure".[7]

The heroic journey classically involves an encounter with, if not passage through, the underworld: Odysseus releases souls out of Erebus, Theseus returns from the Labyrinth, the place of sacrifice and death, Aeneas visits his dead father, Orpheus reclaims Eurydice, Dante passes through the twenty-four circles of Hell to climb Mount Purgatory. Ana Maria Pacheco's work, however, demonstrates more interest in the experience of Pantagruel's squire, Epistemon, whose head is chopped off in a battle with the Giants, *Gargantua and Pantagruel XI.* When his head is stitched back on to his body by Panurge, Epistemon reports that his time in hell was so pleasurable that he was reluctant to return to life. Through his discussions and drinking with the dead ("we tossed it down like theologians") Epistemon establishes that hell is the inverse of each individual's condition in this world. In death, therefore, the rich and powerful lose their wealth and esteem, and the humble are ennobled: Odysseus becomes a 'mower', Hector a 'sauce taster', and Helen a 'placer of chambermaids'. The last two books of Rabelais' novel parody the heroic journey, particularly the quest for the Holy Grail, as Pantagruel and his retinue set out to find the Holy Bottle of Bacbuc. However, when a tyrant parodies the heroic the results can be chilling. Pantagruel relates Herod's plan to be mourned as the hero he is not. Herod arranged to forestall Jewish rejoicing at his death by having all Jewish nobles and magistrates killed at the moment of his own demise: "Then he said to his sister Salome and her husband Alexander: ". . . If this is done all Judea will be mourning and lamenting despite themselves, and strangers will think that it is on account of my death. It will just appear as if some heroic soul has died"."[8]

Pacheco's heroes are unsure of themselves. From the early etchings *The Face of the Hero*, 1976, and drypoints *This Time They came to Stay*, 1978, the figures betray anxiety, fear, anguish. They seem to wear their animal masks/heads as much for protection as to inspire awe. The shepherd cowers before the ram's head in the drypoint *Man and His Sheep II* 1986, as if the power of the deity lies in the mask. The head of the ram-angel in *Revelation I* reminds us that the Lamb of God is part-animal; here it is more like a rat, but instead of eating the book he is feeding it to John of Patmos. Rather he is thrusting it down his throat, as John, who will later utter prophecies over peoples, nations and many kings, stands dwarfed in his playpen/tumbril. Write down all that you have seen: the rat-angel with the blood-soaked arm is choking a child-man with a blood-red book.

The figures in Pacheco's work are as divine and bestial, as frightening and comical as ourselves. In the prints, as with the sculpture, we become involved with the drama as we observe, interpret or narrate events, identify relationships, glances, gestures: everyone is implicated. Looking at the work it may comfort us to identify with the oppressed, even with the bound and tortured figures, for example, in *Quietus est 2* and in *And They Inherited the Earth II,* but we might also recognise ourselves as the tormentors and conspirators in these works.

The fear and intimidation engendered by the abuse of power is reinforced by the relish which some of Pacheco's figures seem to take in other's discomfort, for example, the two standing men in *Some Exercise of Power*, 1980. Similarly, the expressions of two of the suited figures in *The Banquet*, 1985, or of the torturers in *And They Inherited the Earth*, are demonic, projecting us, in Bataille's words, "with greater violence into the vacant night". But we have a power against this, there is a spell against such authoritarian closure if we can invoke it: we can giggle, snigger along with figures in the images, for example, *Terra Ignota 8* and *9*, *Don Quijote y Dulcinea 3* and in

Revelation I, 1993-4

the painting *Memória Roubada I*, 1992. This is not to laugh as fools but to perceive pomposity, ridiculousness and absurdity; to recognise the demonic, destructive as the projection of fear as well as its invocation. The grotesque-horrific may be deflated by the grotesque-satiric, Gargantua pissing on the Parisians, *Gargantua and Pantagruel I*, or the woman frightening the devil by lifting up her skirt, *Gargantua and Pantagruel VIII* and *XIII*. For Mikhail Bakhtin laughter has an essential relation to freedom, for it is potentially non-hierarchical, non-coercive and transgressive; it maintains the possibility of change and banishes the immediate threat. Bakhtin argued that the Middle Ages was the high point in the history of laughter, because then laughter "remained outside all official spheres of ideology and outside all official strict forms of social relations". He situated Rabelais' writing as the most successful example of this tendency: "Rabelais' images have a certain undestroyable, non-official nature. No dogma, no authoritarianism, no narrow-minded seriousness can coexist with Rabelaisian images."[9]

Man and His Sheep I, 1986

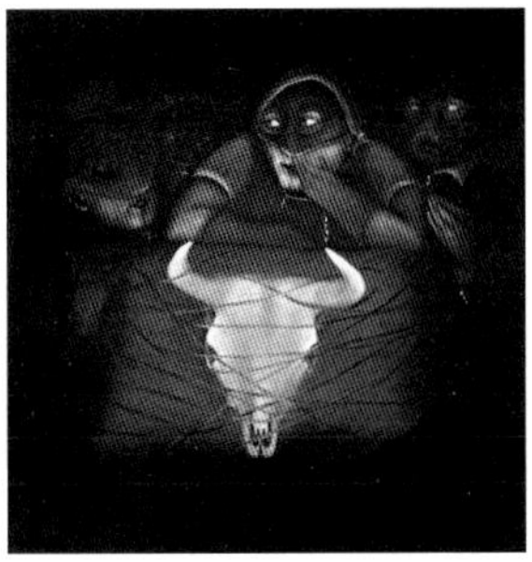

Memória Roubada I, 1992

We should eschew reading Pacheco's work solely through her foreignness, her cultural difference, by positioning her perspective as 'exotic', for this renders our experience of the work as a form of cultural tourism. However, it is important that the work resists assimilation; it expresses estrangement and the fragility of human consciousness rather than any sense of comfort, composure or serenity. In this way it operates in what Edward Said has called "the perilous territory of not belonging". Said has written of the discontinuities, disorientation and solitariness of exiles and has identified creative possibilities in this potentially melancholic state of being. In order to explore this, Said adapted a term from music, suggesting that the experience of the exile produces an awareness that is 'contrapuntal'; that is, able to draw upon and acknowledge the "simultaneous dimensions" of different cultures.[10]

This analysis is very relevant to Pacheco's work. Although not an exile, more accurately an emigré, her experience of the very different cultures of England and Brazil, each a compound of many cultural ingredients, echoes in the many references the work draws upon: classical myth, Brazilian folktale, mystical Catholicism, the fashion catwalk, medieval satire. The work reflects the experience of the outsider, not of the excluded, but of one who can choose or refuse the right to belong. If the entire world is now a foreign land it is, as Theodore Adorno ironically observed: "part of morality not to be at home in one's home".[11]

Notes

1 Hélène Cixous, 'The Author In Truth', in *Coming to Writing and Other Essays*, edited by Deborah Jenson, Harvard, 1991, p.161.
2 James Joyce, *A portrait of the Artist as a Young Man*, Penguin, 1992, p.149.
3 The Latin text was inscribed by Ana Maria Pacheco on an untitled drawing study for painting, 1983 and is repeated on *In Illo Tempore VIII*, oil on gesso, 1994.
4 *No hay quien los socorra*: title of plate 60 of Goya's series of etchings, *The Disasters of War*, 1810-1814.
5 D. H. Lawrence, 'The Ship of Death' in *The Selected Poems of D H Lawrence*, edited by J. Reeves. Heinemann, 1974, p. 83.
6 St John of the Cross, 'Dark Night of the Soul', translated by E. Allison Peers, in *The Complete Works of St. John of the Cross*, Vol. 1, Burns & Oatcs, 1957, pp. 325-6.
7 Theodore Adorno and Max Horkheimer, 'The Parable of the Oarsmen', reprinted in *Art in Theory 1900-1990*, edited by C. Harrison & P. Wood, Blackwell, Oxford, 1992, pp. 633-5.
8 François Rabelais, *The Histories of Gargantua and Pantagruel*, translated by J. M. Cohen, Penguin, 1963, p. 507.
9 Mikhail Bakhtin, *Rabelais and His World*, translated by Helene Iswolsky, MIT, 1968, p. 73, p. 3.
10 Edward Said, 'Reflections on Exile', *Granta* 13, Autumn 1984, Cambridge, UK, pp. 157-172.
11 Theodore Adorno, 'Minima Moralia', *ibid*, p.170.

And They Inherited the Earth II, 1993-4

Quietus est

Dom Antony Sutch

An awareness of the pain of the cross that is life, or rather, as is said, 'to live is to suffer from a disease that only death can cure' causes curses to reign down on birth itself. Would it not have been better for Leviathan to have remained wild, for the world of chaos never to have been tamed, for the primeval irrationality to have remained? These forces are still abroad and they dwell in darkness. If a man of faith yet faces what seems an evil cosmic tyranny, if all that humankind has is an endless set of riddles about being and purpose, if there is no obvious balance of reward and punishment or no measuring rod of justice, is not terror already abroad? Birth becomes the stepping stone from oblivion into the ghastliness of conscious experience. All that remains for time is to be a torrent of pent-up anguish. As has been said of Job so can be said of Pacheco's etching 'let his soliloquy rise as a rhythmic cry of wounded animality.' At birth itself, it would seem that the forces of chaos, of terror lurk to ensure their continued hold upon life itself. Would death be a way of oblivion or is even death merely the refuge of the cry that is the anatomy of despair? The cry of the ecstatic mother giving birth is the moment of the cry of the born expelled from communal protection to isolated embattlement. It is retrospective madness: neither philosophy nor religion seems to have answers until man's finitude is acknowledged, the frustrations of existence accepted and the God whose thoughts are not our thoughts is heard.

The closing over with waters, the experience of drowning conjures a whole gamut of meanings and uses of the symbol and reality of water. The Red Sea, the Jordan, the Dead Sea, the Sea of Galilee: but also the waters that covered the face of the earth before creation – so Jonah. Jonah wilfully disobedient, refusing to enact a command of God to save the lives of the despised foreigner. Pacheco has caught the moment of peace when the fight against compulsive righteous action has been overcome. The calmness and stillness of the inert body, captured almost by thorns and reeds on the sea bed, coming to accept that only righteousness is the alternative to death. The spiritual schooling is complete. Water, the place of Leviathan and chaos; deep, the infinite fears of nihilism and separation.

'Behold the hour is at hand.'

These fateful words. This fateful moment. The moment of destiny. A decisiveness bleak in its startling reality. No escape. The cup is overflowing; life's blood is draining. The gibbet is set, the cart is drawing away to darkness. A mask to cover the terror is in place. An awesome hour.

Even more awesome is the confrontation of death; that death's apparent victory and then its divine vanquishing. The echoes of the old testament in Paul's sublime poem to victory are equally depicted by Pacheco's use of bird-like creatures to represent death and life, failure and success, captivity and freedom. Echoes of joyous communal tribal chanting 'fly like a bird to its mountain' are reverberated in the movement and confrontationalism of Pacheco. Yet here is a bolder conversion statement using apocalyptic imagery, with Paul, to rejoice in the imperishable and immortal. The enclosure of truth forces the direct confrontation of fear and gives a final demonstration of power and of love. There is to be no oblivion. Rather there is a rapturous assurance that death is consumed and even mocked, pitied and seen as an illusion. We have, with Pacheco, an intuitive insight into the secrets of life. Yukio Mishima's words ring true that these things are 'perhaps not discernable through

Quietus est 1, 1993-4

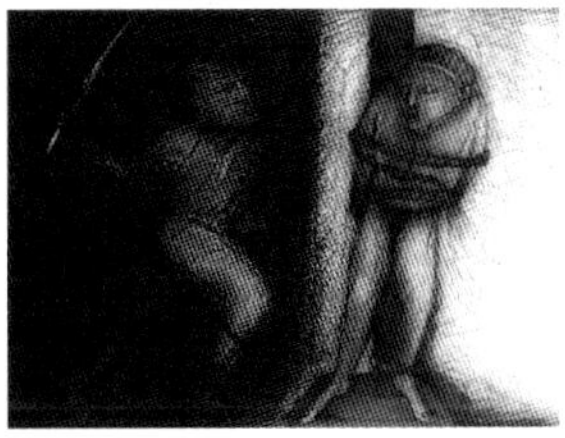

Quietus est 2, 1993-4

◂ *Quietus est 5*, 1993-4, detail

ordinary perception and reason but only through some supernatural power, some extremely accurate, systematic, intuitive super-logic.' Mystery remains mystery but we know there is no sting in death.

In the midst of gloom, in a world shrouded by death, the day of light's epiphany dawns. The radiance of the new rising sun suffuses the world. Light, righteousness, redemption: a rapturous faith and enthusiasm is evoked. Glory and salvation are the central themes and a theophany in fire and light is called up by Isaiah. The dark void of evil is passed, the moral nihilism is replaced by the absolute, anarchy is cleared and vision is assumed. Pacheco, associating closely the symbolic and the spiritual, brings a god out of the darkness, bearing the world, crucified in salvation. Out of the fire, the rubicund dawn of a new era enlightens all.

Quietus est 4, 1993-4 ▾

All is quiet. Be still.

The Work of Ana Maria Pacheco

Andrew Brighton

Ana Maria Pacheco was born in Goiânia, capital of the State of Goiás in Brazil in 1943. She took degrees in both art and music in Goiás, studied music and education at the University of Brazil in Rio de Janeiro, and then taught at both Universities in Goiás before coming to London to study at the University of London Slade School of Art in 1973. Since 1980 she has had a number of one person shows in private and major public galleries in Britain and abroad, and has contributed to important mixed exhibitions.

But this essay is not about Ana Maria Pacheco, it is about her work. It argues a reading of the work by descriptions of what it does and how it does it.

The Language of Bodies

Which way to go next? Uneasy, mouth open, he glances to the right. Naked but for briefs, behind him a flock of seven clothed women look, stare or argue. On this shepherd's crook is the severed head of a ram and his right hand is red. Alone and exposed, he has won his bloody emblem of dominance by butchery but his sheep bicker behind him like spectators at a street fight.

To encounter this group of carved and painted wooden figures that Pacheco has called *Man and His Sheep* (1989) is to join it, to become part of the crowd; as you read the faces and gestures of the figures, the same kind of attention can slip onto other people examining it. In this sense we join the uncertainty of the man and the seven women. Each time I have seen Pacheco's work in a public place I have been aware that, more than is usual in galleries, people talk, exchange observations, report the vivacity of the experience to each other. The work speaks in terms which seem easily recognisable.

To make an understanding of any communicative act requires knowledge. The knowledge needed to start to read Pacheco's work is commonplace. Like waxworks the figures are near life-sized and their colouring life-like. They tell us twice what they are depicting, first as shape and then by applied colour. This double articulation and consequent ease of reading perhaps explains why polychromatic sculpture has been used to address popular audiences; it was used by the church, and still visitors queue to enter Madame Tussaud's waxworks. Of particular relevance to Pacheco is the popular tradition of sculpture in South America. It had its origins in the painted wooden Iberian church carvings imported in the conquest of South America, it joined with indigenous traditions of carving and continues as a folk art.[1] It is popular in the sense that it is a vernacular tradition of making, its representations are clear, it is handmade, technologically basic and belongs to a cultural economy which predates mass production for mass consumption.

Similarly, Pacheco's drawings and prints have an apparent transparency, an ease of recognition. They are essentially linear, use familiar schema, they portray people and actions with a clarity resembling political cartoons. But this clarity should not be mistaken for lack of sophistication. There is more visually going on in Pacheco's work than simply inciting recognition of people and things. On attention the sculptures reveal themselves as carvings with paintings on them; the paint does not simply follow the carved form, it has a life of its own and there is play between paint and shape. Similarly, the virtuoso hatching of the prints assaults the linear structure of the images, just as in the paintings a deep ambiguous darkness surrounds the figures: the apparent

Man and His Sheep, 1989, detail

clarity of the work is threatened by a literal and metaphoric darkness.

What is it we recognise in these relatively transparent works? They begin by calling on our skills at recognising gestures, body stance, facial expression and codes of dress. In other words, those skills we constantly deploy to socially locate and read each other for aggression, approval or desire. We are all literate in the language of bodily expression. However, priorities differ; for instance, a strong six-foot man looks for different signals in the street than a woman alone. The language is not universal; the vocabulary and meaning of gestures change from culture to culture. It is ambiguous without the context of words; agony and ecstasy can look much the same, and it is limited in what can be communicated. But while we may misread, we do still read.

We can read, as it were, the words and sentences, but what is being said? For example, *Man and His Sheep* is not an unambiguous image of male dominance of women, nor does it extol leadership, or, alternatively, the power of the collective. The essential paradox is that Pacheco's work is grounded in popular visual language but has unpopular things to say.

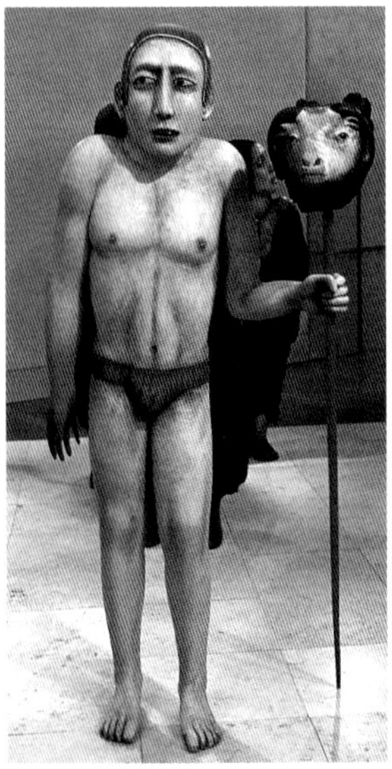

Man and His Sheep, 1989, detail

The Denial of Victims and Paradox

The artist Peter de Francia wrote of Pacheco's work, that it induced "doubts as to the various roles allotted to her protagonists, to the degree of complicity existing between her figures or alternatively of their mutual estrangement. In terms of roles, which one is victim?"[2] In denying us victims the work also denies us heroes and the triumph of good over injustice. How does the work deny us victims? Look at those who might be taken as passive recipients of cruelty. Those with striped knickers are partially ridiculous but then they have teeth. Pacheco inserts false teeth in the mouths of many of her sculptures. They are manufactured for dentists; stained and imperfect, they are made to anonymously fill gaps in blemished families of real teeth. In the sculptures they tend to spill aggressively outwards, following the line of the lips rather than stand back rooted in the upper and lower jaws. These are inhumanly large mouths dominated by an over-abundance of canines and incisors, teeth for ripping and tearing.

In *The Banquet* (1985), for instance, a naked figure lies on a trestle table straight and stiff, stomach, thighs, chest pressed against the table top, fingers splayed, shoulders and head raised, the jaw juts forward, mouth open, eyes rolled back like a frightened animal. Four besuited figures are gathered around the table like self-satisfied executives taking a pub lunch. The naked figure's hands are open as if in some supplicant gesture but its mouth is full of carnivorous teeth. Teeth are ignoble, they are not shown traditionally in paintings of the great, and in the age of film and photography clean straight teeth are dentally engineered for our leaders.

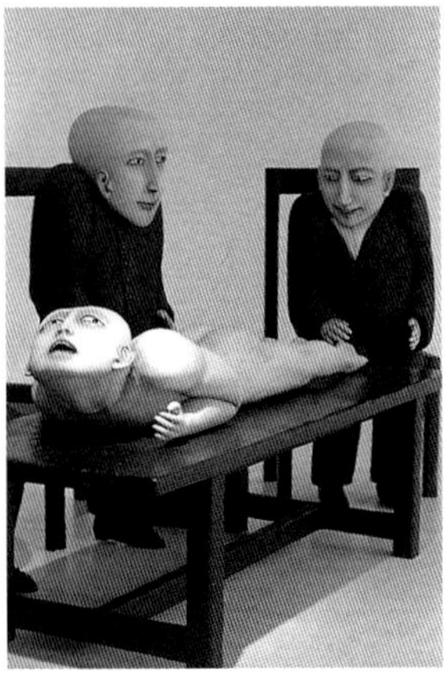

The Banquet, 1985, detail

Crooked, stained teeth are a mark of bestiality, a sign of participation in the cycle of blood and death that sustains carnivorous life. As in Dostoevsky novels, no pure heroes or villains, no innocent victims only different kinds of participation: look at the smiling teeth-crammed mouths of the hanging men in *Acrobats* (1983) and those of some of the women in *Man and His Sheep*: victims too have had their moments of cruelty.

"Practically all the concepts upon which her sculptures are based are concerned with paradox", de Francia further observes of Pacheco's work. A requirement for a paradoxical statement in the initial sense of the word, a statement contrary to received opinion, is that it must imply the opinion, belief or logic it contradicts. Wordsworth's "the child is father to the man" plays upon conventional ideas of child, father, man.

Pacheco's work implies the banal. The language of bodily expression is a component of banal culture, it is part of the culture we must all learn to be competent members of society. We are taught to eat, dress, act and speak in ways that communicate primarily our normality. To be functioning members of modern society we must also be competent consumers of mass culture, we must be able to understand the conventions of administration, advertising, news and entertainment. The illiterates of banal culture are described as idiots, as subnormal or handicapped. Why call this shared culture banal? Because the etymology of the word provides an analogy: in origin 'banal' meant compulsory and common services demanded by the feudal state. For example, peasants were required to have the wheat they grew ground in the banal mill, the mill belonging to the lord; for this a toll was extracted. The toll paid for banal culture is all-encompassing; how we think and feel, how we conceive of ourselves, what we know and value is formed in this common and compulsory culture. It is this banal culture that provides the harmonics, the conventions, the codes, in which modern art has made discord and difference.

Acrobats, 1983, detail

How does Pacheco's work counter banality given that it calls upon the banal language of bodily expression? As we walk around her life-sized figures our companions in the gallery provide the norm. As I have said, our reading of body language may slip onto other visitors but we do not mistake them for one of Pacheco's figures. Characteristically these have over-large heads for their bodies, rounded shoulders and thick legs; they have, in other words, some of the characteristics of babies' and children's bodies. In many of the paintings, drawings and etchings, people are costumed as for a game, they crowd together with the intimacy of children, hands are put over mouths to hide a snigger or wonder, they glance guiltily or malevolently out at the viewer as if an adult has stumbled on their tainted charade. Often there is something humorous about these creatures. But these child-like personages are of adult height, and in both the images and the sculptures they have the physical attributes of adult sexuality.

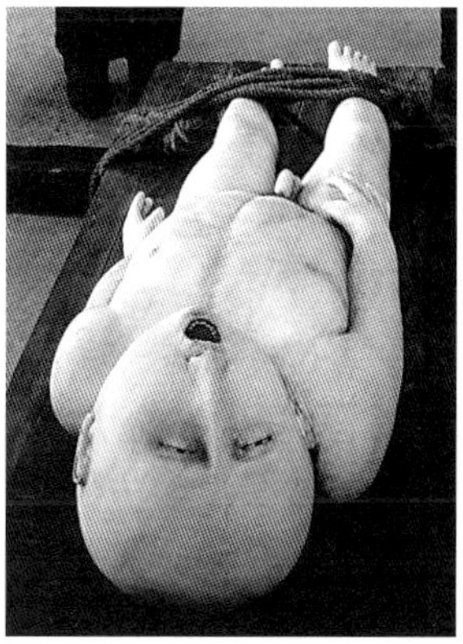

Some Exercise of Power 1980, detail

These adult-infants are disturbing. The games that they play are caricatures of adult rituals: like politicians they address crowds, like philosophers they converse, like scientists they examine strange specimens, and like artists they show off skills. A sense of the infantile motives beneath the skin of adult socialisation suggests that politics, philosophy, science and art are re-enactments of pre-pubescent gropings, torture games and fantasies. The adult world is infantile desire, polymorphous perversity to use Freud's term, that has learnt the camouflage of social rituals. "The child is father to the man."

Making an Imaginary

It is important for my understanding of Pacheco's work not to see it as simply depictions of the injustices of Brazilian society. To read it as an exotic folk art or liberal political protest is to deny it its seriousness. The work is inserted into the context of international modern art, and it is in the discourse of serious art that the work's complexity can be elaborated.

Man and His Sheep, 1989, detail

So for instance, in *Man and His Sheep* and in many of the pictures, women wear the black and shawls of Latin countries where peasant culture and the proprieties of the traditional Catholic church are still strong. While they may be derived and schematised from the garb of Pacheco's Brazilian youth, in the context of modern urban culture they function to alienate the figures from the normal dress, to remove them from mere reportage and the familiar realist conventions of entertainment. For instance, the sculpture becomes parochial if imagined in conventional Western dress. Rather than alluding to the specifics of Brazilian society, the costume's function is to suggest a universality, like classical costumes in paintings of ancient and biblical mythological history, i.e., History Painting. The work constitutes an imaginary; a fictive form of life which serves as a mythology, it evokes a complex of relationships and practices. In my reading, this imaginary is a critical or paradoxical mirror. Rather than reflecting back the normality of appearance, it requires guilty knowledge for recognition. Guilty because in recognising this imaginary, many of the resemblances to our world are, as I have suggested above, at least uncomfortable.

The Head and the Severed Head

Unlike History Painting, Pacheco's work rarely has a fixed iconography. In other words, there is usually no single narrative text which identifies particular figures or objects with specific meanings. Rather, Pacheco's work develops an iconographic idiolect, a particular use of symbols, motifs and devices which have a number of connotations and together constitute the work's imaginary.

For instance, the recurring device of isolated heads. In the three-dimensional work they evoke but diverge from a number of sculptural types. *Study of Head* (1990) and *Study of Head for Requiem* (1989) resemble the remains of larger works as in the head of a Buddha or the colossal basalt heads of ancient Mexico. They suggest Pacheco's imaginary has a past of which these idealised heads are memorials. Alternatively, *Study of Head* (1989) is closer to a gargoyle. The character of *Studies of Heads* (1986) and *Box of Heads* (1984) suggest a waxwork museum of the evil humours; they have the vitality of angry and vindictive persons deprived of their bodies displayed in a freak show.

The device of the isolated head extends into the motif of the severed head. In the drypoint *Man and His Sheep I* of 1986, the ram-headed shepherd stands over his gaggling flock confined in hatched darkness out of which emerges strings of control which he holds lightly between forefinger and thumb of his gloved hand. In the drypoint *Man and His Sheep II*, the ram's head stands on a pole, and what I have called the string of control leads from the head and disappears stage right. The shepherd glances behind him as he, exposed without the mask of power, approaches the head.

Man and His Sheep II, 1986 ▸

I read the iconographic idiolect of *Man and His Sheep* drypoints and sculptures as an allegory of power. Pacheco's symbol for domination in this reading is connotatively complex but it suggests that leadership is animal and irrational. The ram's head is horned and masculine, it brings together sexuality and violence; it is a decapitated head, it is created out of butchery. Spiked on a pole it resembles a processional staff, a grim crozier, and like a flag it commands loyalty. But a head on a spike is also a mode of displaying the executed; power needs its martyrs. To be led is to be bound by a kind of atavistic enchantment.

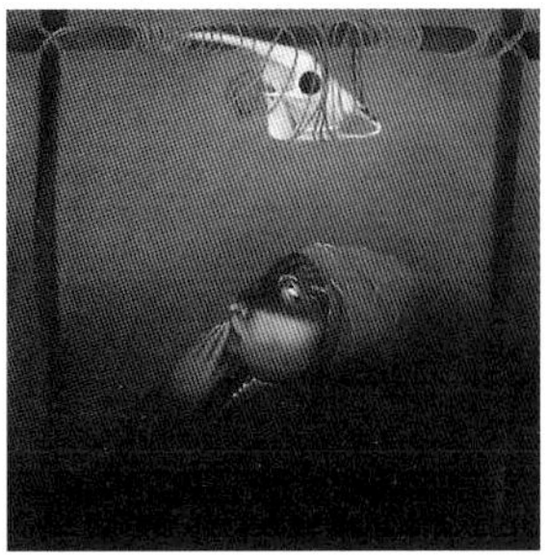

Memória Roubada II, 1992

The motif of isolated head or skull appears in the six paintings Pacheco made in 1992, the year in which Columbus' 'discovery' of the Americas was celebrated. Seen from the perspective of the native Americans who predated Columbus, there was little to celebrate. In that year Pacheco made six paintings, the title *Memória Roubada* is a quotation from lines written by a friend on the conquest of South America.

Memória Roubada

Shot in the ears
Severed hands
Poked eyes
Castrated sexes [3]

The words speak not just of the brutality of the conquest but of the attack upon the memory, the history, the consciousness that preceded and remembered the invasion; a culture deafened, crippled, blinded, castrated and still the brutalised subject of modern imperialism. The formation of an understanding of the past is still bound in with the continuities of imperialism. In one painting a figure looks up at a sheep's skull tied to a cross-beam, the shape of the observer's head and that of the skull is the same. The string that ties the skull to the beam also secures the head-dress of the viewer. In another of the paintings the pig dangling from ribbons is the marionette of one of the masked spectators. The two paintings in the series which depict single severed human heads, one hanging from a rope, the other spiked, are painted with the kind of smooth transitions from dark to light typical of sub-Raphael paintings of the head of Christ to be found in Catholic churches. Christ is usurped by the heads of the victims of Christian imperialism in the pictorial language of Christian piety.

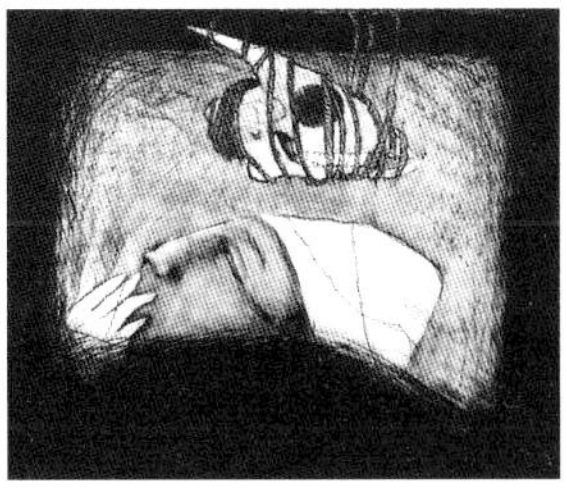

Wisdom of Old Age II, 1985

Iconographic Lexicon

The imaginary of Pacheco's work is then complex, it brings together a number of sometimes paradoxical connotations. This is true even in the case of works that do have a known textual source. Frances Carey, in her essay *The Prints of Ana Maria Pacheco*, records that the title of the series of 1981 etchings *Every Man Wears a Head on His Shoulder* has its source in Penderecki's opera *The Devils of Loudun.* "The remark in the opera is made à propos of the head of a criminal which a surgeon and a chemist have contrived to purchase after the body has been cut down from the gallows."[4] In Pacheco's prints the heads seem to be alive, they eye the viewer out of their confined space. Sinister and threatening seen in the light of their titles' textual allusion they suggest the theme of the guilty victim.

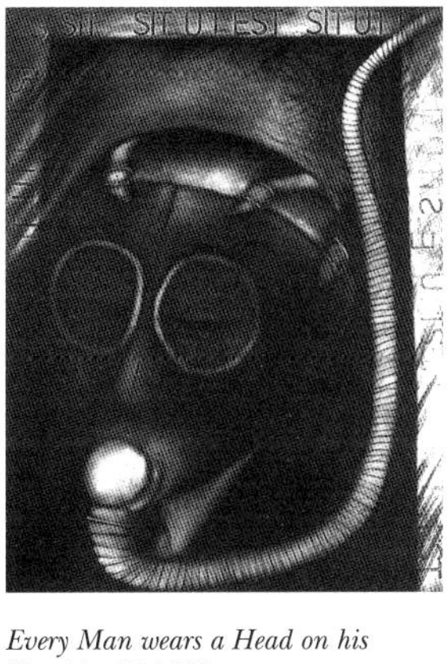

Every Man wears a Head on his Shoulder IV, 1981

However, there are the traditional iconographic connotations of the motif of the severed head. For instance, Perseus beheaded the Gorgon Medusa and used her terrible visage to turn Phineus and his followers to stone, and St. Paul was one of many beheaded and much depicted Christian martyrs. The principal echo implied in

Beheaded (Salome), study for painting, 1991

Beheaded (Judith), study for painting, 1991

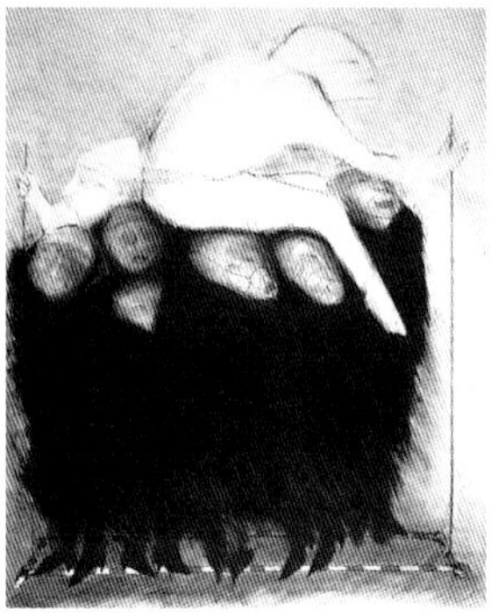

The Endeavours of a Certain Poet, 1984

Pacheco's use of the motif, which eventually becomes explicit in some works, is beheadings involving women using their sexual power: the stories of Judith and of Salome. In both cases the key figure is a widow, a woman who has known men and their desires and has become independent, but it is also a conspiracy of women rather than just a woman: Judith and her servant beheaded Holofernes, and Salome was Herodias' means of tricking Herod into beheading St. John the Baptist.

In 1991 Pacheco drew some studies for paintings entitled *Beheaded,* and she associates them by additional bracketed tiles with the stories of both Judith and Salome. Exceptionally an iconographic source is identified in these titles, but the stories are transformed in Pacheco's iconographic idiolect. *Beheaded (Salome)* I read as amalgamation and transformation of two moments in the story of John the Baptist. The scene is primarily that of the Baptism of Christ in the river Jordan, but the figure of Christ here is Salome. Rather than the Holy Ghost descending from heaven as a dove, Herodias descends on a trapeze to whisper in Salome's ear. The figure of John the Baptist holding the staff of authority has become the horrified Herod, and in the water of Jordan is a ram's head. Read as this enfolding of the stories, the Baptism becomes an initiation into power and guilt, there is no innocence or transcendence.

Perhaps until we consider where it puts us, the least ambiguous of Pacheco's works is the carved head of *John the Baptist III* (1992). The sculpture consists simply of a wooden plate held at table height by a single rod, on the plate is a severed head. But as in *Man and His Sheep* we not only see the sculpture, we join it. We are placed in the position of Herod, the head is offered to us. In Pacheco's work the spectator and the crowd are not innocent. When they appear in paintings and prints they are often masked, they too play out roles in the charade of power relations.

The masks take various forms, wire muzzles in the drawing *The Endeavours of a Certain Poet* (1984), gas masks and goggles in *Beheaded (Judith),* but there is one mask which covers the whole face with holes cut around the mouth and eyes; it appears in a number of works including the Judith drawing and in the group around the bull's skull in one of the *Memória Roubada* paintings. The doubled eyes and mouth echo the Aztec carvings of Xipe Totec. In Aztec belief humankind had responsibility for maintaining the Sun, the Earth, the Moon and the Gods of Vegetation and Animal life; human blood was the means of annual rejuvenation. "In the Spring months, at planting time, a youth chosen to represent Xipe was sacrificed and flayed. His skin was then worn as a costume by a living person, as a symbolic enactment of the live seed within the dead husk."[5]

I do not think it helps to read the figures with this particular mask as Xipe Totec, "our Lord the Flayed One"; rather, the resemblance points to another connotation, another resonance which runs through Pacheco's iconographic idiolect. This is the theme of the crowd's, the group's, society's demand for leaders that are both masters and victims offered up for the rejuvenation of the patterns of power, the charades, which order social relationships.

Conclusion: Politics and Strategy

In this reading of Pacheco's work it is overtly political; it is about power in society. Helen Boorman put it well in her essay on Pacheco when she wrote, "Ana takes on the complexity and duplicity of power itself. Mediating the Orthodoxy of Catholicism and Foucaultian analysis her work exposes internal, mythological forces, the unconscious, sexuality, the hidden psyche as well as their surface manifestations, sadism, abuse, cruelty and fear."[6]

An essay different to this one would locate her work in the context of recent art. I can only try to do this briefly here. In a culture dominated by the mass means of communication, art as a communicative activity or as an activity concerned with the means of communication, necessarily has political significance. Pacheco and many artists of her generation and younger who are informed by cultural theory are well aware of the politics of culture. The more usual strategy arising from this political awareness uses combination and juxtaposition to defamiliarise the dominant conventions of representation. It criticises, as it were, the grammar of the dominant culture by re-combining its elements and thus exposing its ideological norms. I am thinking of the work of Robert Gober and Cindy Sherman for example.

Pacheco's strategy is different. She works with fiction, myth and metaphor rather than combination and context. Pacheco uses popular traditions rather than mass culture or for that matter traditionalist sculptural figuration. By these means the work has escaped some of the ideological baggage of both the dominant means of representation and of traditionalist European figurative sculpture and painting. She has elaborated an imaginary in which can be recognised the shamanism of leadership and those exercises of power which constitute social life. The work's elaborated iconography constructs a theatre of social relations. In this theatre there are no innocents, to enter society is to play in the charade. In its apparent accessibility the work might be said to be democratic but seen as images of society, at the very least, it questions the value of democracy as we know it. Perhaps it points to power as the given, the original sin, of society itself.

I can read no images of hope into the work. There is, however, a final paradox in how the work places its viewers, what it asks of us. By entering its imaginary, recognising its escapes from banality and thus its black humour, its accusations and satire, the viewer is seduced into reflective effort. The work assumes and creates a disenchanted intelligence. In that, it can be said, lies its hope.

Notes

1 *Baroque to Folk*, Museum of International Folk Art, Santa Fe, USA, 1980.
2 Peter de Francia, *Some Exercise of Power.* Exhibition Guide, Camden Arts Centre, London, 1991.
3 José Lobo: 'Chumbo nos ouvidos, màos arrancadas, olhos vazados, sexos castrados'.
4 Frances Carey, 'The Prints of Ana Maria Pacheco', *Print Quarterly*, Vol.V, No.3, September 1988, p.277.
5 George Kubler, *The Art and Architecture of Ancient America*, Penguin Books, Harmsworth, 1962, p.l9.
6 Helen Boorman, 'Unfolding the Magic Spell: Imagery and Imagination in the Work of Ana Maria Pacheco', *Ana Maria Pacheco: Sculpture, Paintings, Drawings and Prints 1980-1989*, Pratt Contemporary Art, 1989, p.9.

Ana Maria Pacheco

Frances Carey

The startling individuality of Ana Maria Pacheco's work makes it hard to comprehend the travail she once experienced in trying to evolve a distinctive artistic vocabulary of her own, yet this struggle lies at the heart of the dramatic tension embodied in her compositions. It was Pacheco's translation to this country from Brazil, in 1973, which proved critical for the development of her imagery. She came from the interior of Brazil, as a practising sculptor, to study under Reg Butler at the Slade; the dramatic change in her environment, however, provoked such a sense of dislocation and deracination that Pacheco considers it took seven years for her to find an appropriate means of expression in her sculpture; the resolution of her difficulties in this area finally emerged in 1980 in a group of three polychromed wooden figures called *Some Exercise of Power*, her first titled piece of sculpture.

In the course of seeking a way out of her impasse, Pacheco extended the whole range of her working practice by developing the role of printmaking and drawing vis-à-vis her sculpture. She resorted to printmaking, initially, just as a temporary diversion from the more intractable problems of a three-dimensional medium and her first attempts were largely reproductive of her sculptural work. However, she quickly perceived the opportunities printmaking afforded for prolonged experimentation with a wide variety of ideas which could be more easily assimilated to a two-dimensional surface. Between 1976 and 1980 Ana Maria Pacheco completed nearly twenty distinctive groups of etchings whose physical execution became analogous to the reductivist activity of carving, the method she had adopted by 1980 as her preferred means of sculptural expression. Pacheco talks about 'discovering' the image buried beneath layers of aquatint on her etching plates, a process akin to the carver's attempt to release or reveal the subject imprisoned within the block of wood or stone.

"But one of the things I learnt through all these years is that the technique is not that difficult. The difficulty is to find a way to translate your concept, ideas, to find a language." By 1980 Pacheco had clearly attained a new articulacy, revealing a latent Latin American sensibility which appears to have been accentuated by her sojourn in England. Throughout the current decade she has increased the scope of her ambition on both a conceptual and a formal level, culminating, for the moment, in the two monumental compositions which are the focus of this exhibition. The dramatic freedom which Pacheco first discovered in printmaking during the latter part of the 1970s has subsequently emerged in drawings, pastels and oil paintings as a parallel activity to her sculpture. *Man and His Sheep* has evolved through this type of activity over a period of four years, after the initial idea came from a competition on the theme of world peace. In the prints and drawings Pacheco has variously introduced the sheep as draped around the principal figure's shoulders, and as a head either borne aloft on a pole or substituted for the head of the main protagonist; the resultant hybrid creature, in the latter case, recalls the minotaur on the right of Picasso's great etching of 1935, *The Minotauromachia*. The symbolic role of Pacheco's hybrid may also contain echoes of that ascribed to the blind minotaur in Picasso's work where it represents, on one level, artistic vision; the creature is unable to see the natural world yet in the darkness of the labyrinth can pierce what remains impenetrable to mortal eye. The reference to the sheep in Pacheco's composition introduces a sacrificial element but we are left uncertain as to whether the sacrifice is part of a redemptive process. The ideas involved still await further clarification in the artist's own mind.

Man and His Sheep, 1989

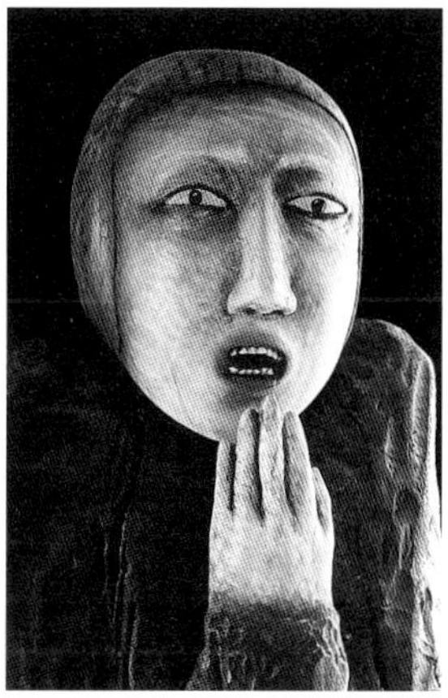

Man and His Sheep, 1989, detail

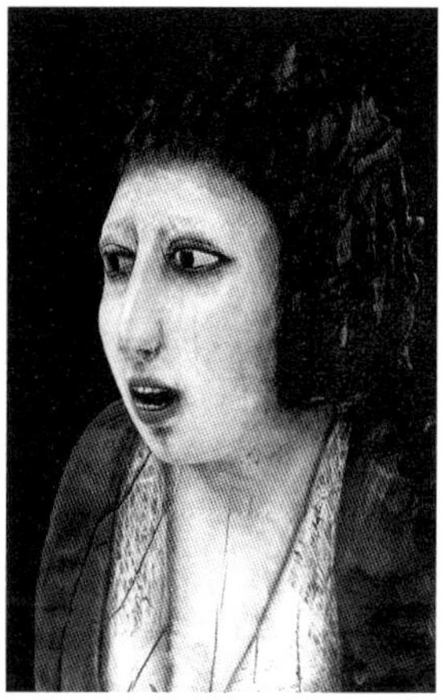

Man and His Sheep, 1989, detail

◂ *Man and His Sheep*, 1989, detail

Requiem, study for sculpture, 1986

With *Requiem*, on the other hand, the artist felt the idea was complete but not the execution when it was first displayed at the Stoke-on-Trent National Garden Festival in 1986. The composition was partly conceived as a homage to Pacheco's father yet it is not dissimilar in structure to *Man and His Sheep*, the people in this case, according to the artist, being concealed within the pile of stones.

The intense physical exertion required for the making of Pacheco's sculpture is not merely a means to an end but an essential part of the creative process. One of her assistants on *Requiem* at Stoke-on-Trent conveyed this point when she described how "the artist worked single-mindedly, coupling intense concentration with exhausting physical labour, creating an atmosphere of momentum that forged the work into existence; . . . Our physical struggle became a vital part of the realisation of a work concerned with an evolving . . . a resolving . . . a breaking-through."[1] Pacheco's iconography is always disturbing; there are no comfortable conclusions to be drawn from her compositions, whose meaning is never quite clear. Her audience, however, needs no careful adumbration of visual metaphors in order to respond to the force of her artistic personality, as demonstrated in 1984 by the enormous success of Pacheco's period of residence in a comprehensive school in Warwickshire. A visiting head teacher wrote an eloquent account of the impact achieved by the artist both in person and through her sculpture, *The Banquet*, which provided the focus for the children's own work:

"Ana had given an introductory talk during which she described how she had had the idea for *The Banquet* fifteen years ago but had only now felt that she was ready to tackle it. Like all sincere art it contains many themes. It shows good and evil, power and ineffectuality, government over people, dictatorship over helpless peasantry, rich devouring poor, wrong conquering and presiding. She was demonstrating very forcibly a personal exploration of an idea, a feeling, an issue that concerned her as an individual and as a member of society, and she was doing it through the medium of wood. She was showing that art is not a remote, mysterious, insubstantial thing, but a serious commitment to effort and achievement . . . This had been my first experience of personal contact with a sculptor and her work, and I had found it overwhelming."[2]

Notes:

1 Sarah Webb, 1986
2 Maureen Allison, Church Lawford First School, Warwickshire, 1984.

Unfolding the Magic Spell: Imagery and Imagination in the work of Ana Maria Pacheco

Helen Boorman

The half-formed figures, gathered in one corner of the large, softly lit garage studio, seem oblivious of any intrusion. Watching, in silence, one can almost hear the rise and fall of voices as they lean towards and away from each other like the members of a Greek chorus, both participants and voyeurs, accusers and accused, oppressors and victims. Their anxious yet conspiratorial whispers become tangible as imagined sounds are echoed in slightly uncomfortable postures. These are figures which are both graceful and awkward. A tall man looks over his shoulder while another covers his mouth with horror, or shame. The smallest, stoutest woman in the group glances up at him, her eyes, pupils extended, suggest curiosity and apprehension. Although she is timeless, both real and mystical, her solid, Roman-sandalled feet stand firmly rooted to the ground. Never quite meeting our gaze, the figures seem shifty. Watchful of one another, the circular grouping nevertheless confirms the dependency of the individuals upon one another.

The figures belong to Ana's most recent large-scale sculpture *Man and His Sheep*. Like much of her work, this new piece seems straightforward but its iconography is complex, and not only because its elements of irony and ambiguity discourage any single reading. Characteristically, aspects of many different earlier images and sculptures have re-emerged, like intruders whose final presence seems to surprise their own creator Here, the Man we encounter in earlier drawings, wearing the sheep like a stole around his shoulders and who, in a series of drypoints, wears a sheep's-head mask, appears as both shepherd and magician. Through the uncanny merging of pagan and Christian symbolism, a saviour/conjurer is created who acts as the director of fate as well as its victim. In the related drawings, the sheep symbol has merged with the female figure, to give birth to creatures that are magical and satanic. In the sculpture the synthesis of staff/wand, woman and sheep results in an ambiguous attribute which can be read as magician's wand, familiar, jester's staff or mask as well as a symbol of sexuality or innocence. We are taunted by the fact that the lamb, with its metaphorical overtones of sacrifice for the redemption of the soul and the expulsion of evil on earth, is here, itself, an accomplice in a pagan and magical ritual. The sheep's-head wand performs the vital role in the casting of the spell which unfolds in the work.

To this extent, the sculpture *Man and His Sheep* recalls the emotional as well as iconographical content of earlier works, such as the series of ten drypoints *Trust Betrayed*,and bears a close relation to the six drypoints, *A Little Spell in Six Lessons.* In these series, as so often in Ana's work, humans assume the satirical guise of animals, and the underlying themes of cruelty, uncertainty and control surface in each image like a jab from a tiny knife These haunting and intensely memorable images bear witness to a particular sensibility which recognises the extent to which apparently ordinary objects, people and situations can, in an instant, inexplicably and sometimes imperceptibly, as if, indeed in a magical spell, be transformed into the extraordinary.

A Little Spell in Six Lessons 1, 1988

A Little Spell in Six Lessons 2, 1988

Where is man to place his trust?

Because of its intentional iconographic instability, much of Ana's art implies that betrayal is an inevitable part not only of social and institutional life but also of personal and private relations. Nevertheless, the humanity of Ana's work, the strong

The Banquet, 1985

sense that her art neither judges nor censors, suggests a spiritual optimism, a forgiving realism that a more complacent imagery would be unable to attain. An almost childlike fascination, combined with a mischievous enjoyment of the magical spell, bestows on the often painfully charged work a kind of innocence.

Her resistance of any simple polarity makes the placing of Ana's work within any clear moral, religious or political context difficult. Most of the time the work, like its author, is deliberately and frustratingly elusive. Often, the moral content of the work seems as devious and shifty as its central characters. Its ambiguity certainly places it outside the realm of conventionally political art. It is as if the myths and narratives of classical mythology and Catholicism are both redeployed and subverted to comment on but never to elucidate political themes.

If less overtly to do with corruption and cruelty as *The Banquet*, which takes as its starting point the macabre story of *The Devils of Loudun*, works like *Some Exercise of Power* and *Man and His Sheep* bring to light what Ana terms 'the little murders' that underpin the 'civilised' fabric of life. References to international political and moral corruption, or to incidents which she has witnessed and experienced in Brazil, are thus implicit rather than explicit in a piece as disturbing as *The Banquet* or in the series of etchings from 1981, *Every Man Wears a Head on his Shoulder*, the Devil cannot be believed even when he is telling the truth.

Every Man Wears a Head on His Shoulder III, 1981

In *Man and His Sheep*, the attitude of the crowd, in a narrative both mythological and archetypal, adds subtly to the mood of unease and uncertainty. The group we encounter are as suspicious of their own number as they are of the stranger who seems part of and yet not of the crowd. If, as Pacheco herself feels, the Baroque display which characterises Brazilian aesthetics makes 'pure' classicism impossible, the human and moral content of classical theatre is as strong in her work as the suggestion of the Greek chorus in its composition. One has the sense that it is through ignorance, with the pretence of innocence, that the central character finds himself at the mercy of the 'mob' whose initial curiosity turns quickly into jealousy or fear, and whose mixed emotions are ultimately dominated by the more primal desire to hurt and destroy. The work throws the spectator into positions of both identification and alienation so that we are always forced to confront manifestations of our own expectations, prejudices and anxieties.

In this sense, Ana is right to resist a feminist reading of her work. Her female figures have teeth as sharp and as numerous as the male figures, although the 'dangerous games' of the former are more discreet. Her imagery which, like pagan mythology as well as certain branches of recent critical theory, accepts the reality of masks, of multiple and unstable personalities, has a wry self-irony.

A number of works contain elements of self-portraiture and self-caricature which raise powerful issues about the ways in which we see ourselves and the ways that others see us. Her visual narratives echo the form of the novel where the author is both present in, and disguised by, the text. Transposing story into stage, she moves playfully through the work swapping voices and costumes with her cast. Other 'fictitious' characters in the work hint at their 'real' origins. It's hard not to wonder if anyone examining the characters closely will recognise a gesture or posture that feels uncomfortably familiar Many of the texts themselves have the quality of the fairy-tale which teaches us that "the wisest thing . . . is to meet the forces of the mythical world with cunning and high spirits".[1]

Man and His Sheep, study for sculpture, 1986

This is not to say that Ana's work does not ask important questions about human and gender relations. Her self-consciously fetishistic female figures, with their tightly laced boots and clawed gloves, play not only with their opponents but with the discourses of sexuality, objectification and power. The flirtatious gestures and uneasy postures of the female figures in *The Three Graces*, for example, offer a parody of their own objectification. The work, like the more recent *Dangerous Games*, denies and mocks the purely passive role of the feminine in any mythological or contemporary narrative. The sheep-woman confirms the active and magical powers that she often celebrates in women.

The Three Graces 3, 1984

In works like *Acrobats* or *Some Exercise of Power*, nakedness, rather than femaleness, signifies vulnerability. Although the bulky and uniformly suited male figures in the latter, exactly resembling the ghouls in *The Banquet*, are archetypes of patriarchy and oppression, their watchfulness hints at the uncertain alliances which emerge in *Man and His Sheep*, and the predators seem as weak as their naked victims. In these private and public dramas nobody is absolved. By implication, those among us that keep some semblance of innocence are subject to the most ruthless forms of destruction. This is the tragic as much as magic realism which emerges through the recurrent narrative themes of Pacheco's work where the dominant emotions are fear, guilt, fascination and repression.

Never simply rhetorical, Ana takes on the complexity and duplicity of power itself. Mediating the orthodoxy of Catholicism and Foucaultian analysis, her work exposes internal, mythological forces, the unconscious, sexuality, the hidden psyche as well as their surface manifestations – sadism, abuse, cruelty and fear. The *amor carnalis* suggested by attributes like the lighted candle, the fan and the whip, continues to remind us that virtue is fragile. The precariousness of the flame or of the figure on the high wire suggests also that vice and virtue, good and evil cannot easily be distinguished from one another. Life, like the juggled money-bags in *Dangerous Games 2*, can often be confused by random and illogical forces.

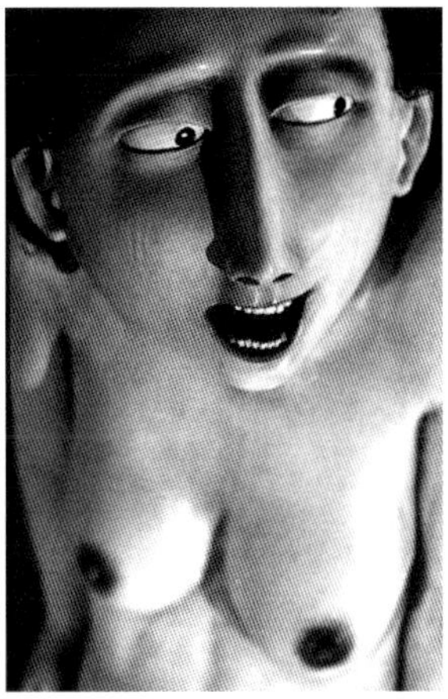

The Three Graces, Figure III, 1983, detail

In keeping with the complexity of the iconography and the narrative, Ana's work draws stylistically on a number of interwoven traditions. The fact that the sculpted figures are painted continues an analogy with the classical period, although their distortion and exaggeration is more reminiscent of folk or medieval art. Although highly expressive, her work is free of the kind of psychological hysteria and narcissism which often mars European expressionism, although a sculptor like Ernst Barlach comes to mind. Other critics have remarked on the sombre Catholicism of the work whose occasionally funereal overtones have recently been lightened by the deliberate use of the resonant colours of medieval stained glass and painted carvings.

For me, although the comparison may seem contrived, the religious mysticism, as well as the theatrical quality of Ana's work, evokes the visually powerful, hypnotic and almost unbearably moving performances of the Polish artist Tadeusz Kantor whose themes of childhood and memory, Catholicism and ritual, institutional and political oppression, share the fascination and ambivalence of Pacheco's. The rituals recalled and re-enacted are those of creation and apocalypse – passion and requiem – which both define the parameters of life and imprison us within them. They permit the unknown as much as they confirm belief or faith. Although, unlike Kantor's plays, Ana's sculpture does not use music, much of her work contains musical and operatic resonances: the chanting of the liturgy, the themes of passion and requiem, attest to the importance of music in the suspension of rationality and in the theatre of the imagination. In the recent work, the sense of religious mystery or ritual, punishment, mourning and transcendence is made poignant by the burning of the figures which not only shapes their garments but brings them into existence.

Dangerous Games 2, 1989

Much of Ana's work reveals her acute sensitivity to both visual and verbal language; symbolism, metaphor, inscription and titling are vital components, all of which allow

The Three Graces: Figure I, study for sculpture, 1983

her to articulate ideas and concepts rooted in ambiguity. She often makes use of medieval Latin inscriptions which serve to enhance the work and often add a further level of meaning or an unexpected dimension. Most refer to the central themes of Ana's work and convey her interest in both the poetic, haunting sounds of the Latin language and its religious and mystical meanings: *Ego genero lumen sed tenebrae meae naturae sunt* (I generate light but darkness is part of my nature).[2] Like the world of appearances the structure of language contains its own elliptical references and Ana's work engages directly with the way in which language is composed of its own semantic and cultural codes. She is aware of the degree to which her move to England and the inevitable comparisons raised between the Portuguese and English languages enhanced her sensitivity to social discourse, humour and irony. The animal figures in *A Little Spell in Six Lessons*, for example, serve as metaphors of the tentative approaches, 'sniffing out', smiles, bites and snarls, which characterise the way in which humans, like animals, test one another. They tease that once the surface veneer of social life, of manners and polite discourse are stripped away, man and beast share in the games of unconscious ritual.

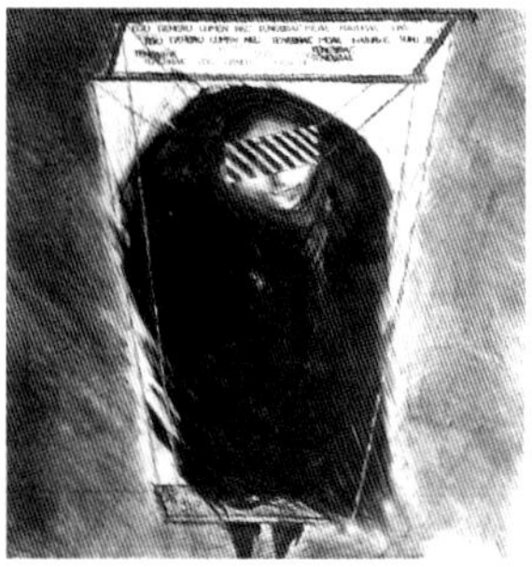

Untitled, study for painting, 1983

In Ana's work the links between death, power, magic and sexuality are strong. Often the sculptures and images recall ancient rites and indicate the extent to which her sensitivity to myth and language is informed by her interest in Carl Jung. Much of the warmth and optimism in her work arises from the fact that her world is not one where the individual is isolated but, rather, woven into the fabric of myth, history, family and community. The associations of the work with medieval roving actors or with the wandering shows which form the subject of much of Márquez's work recall Ana's own stories of her childhood and of the games played by children in the evening sunlit streets of her home town Goiás. In these streets, fantasy, so much a part of Brazilian culture, could find expression, freed from the elements of psychodrama or nightmare fostered by contemporary science fiction. The lighted candles recall the real and fantasy world of childhood: their use at a time of electricity shortages as well as the excitement and fear of the familiar world transformed by candlelight.

A Little Spell in Six Lessons 6, 1988

Ana's creatures walk alongside the carnival but belong to a secret world beneath the surface unearthed. Mysterious and disturbing, they are also her friends. One senses that they are still present in the unmasking at evening and enter into the security of the village or family. The sense of the party, of the dream unfolding, of the ultimate absurdity of the game, reminds one strongly of Fellini, a director whom Ana much admires. Much of the content of her work, as in a cinematic *mise-en-scène*, is offstage, suggested by the characters in the drama and its evocation of fantasy and a momentarily shared world of illusion. Thus, the spectator is invited into the world which Ana creates, to enjoy its richness and to consider its meaning. It is her great achievement that, even as strangers to that world, we are seduced by and moved by its elements of tragedy and comedy. Ana creates a magical space with echoes of church, street corner and theatre where the dramas of the human condition and imagination are performed.

Notes:

1 Walter Benjamin, 'The Story Teller' in *Illuminations*, edited by Hannah Arendt, Shocken Books, New York, 1969, p.102.

2 From Rosarium Philosophorum, believed to be by Hermes.

Ana Maria Pacheco – 'Inventing the Black Powder': Art and Education

Ian Starsmore

Ana Maria Pacheco first came to Norwich School of Art ten or more years ago to give a lecture about her work. It was fascinating to hear her speak of the importance of the folk and popular art traditions in Brazil, and to recognise her as someone who looked at the popular arts with serious eyes. In 1985 Ana applied for the post of Head of Fine Art and came to the School for the pre-interview. She seemed watchful and had a sort of 'what am I getting into' face, as well she might. We looked at a catalogue of 'Spitting Image' photographs and seemed to agree that there were elements of caricature at the edge of her work. For four years afterwards we worked together at Norwich School of Art, as part of a group of people trying to think about what art education might be. Ana always worked frenetically in the college, staying most days until nine or ten in the evenings, stopping only, vanishing only, to prepare work for her exhibitions, often working for four or five days and nights continuously with little or no sleep. Her adventures surrounding the Stoke-on-Trent Garden Festival were as extraordinary as she, Susan O'Toole and Sarah Webb sculpted through sleet, rain and wind, carried generators and were attacked by flying scaffolding.

At the School we evolved a programme of studies which placed an emphasis on the integrity and equal validity of theory and practice. Students in the Fine Art Department will testify to the number of times that Ana would challenge them if they were in the studio and there was a lecture or seminar they were to attend. We worked to make what I think is an un-English pattern, to bring together scholarship and creativity. The models for this can be found more in literary criticism and theory. Seamus Heaney writing of Wordsworth suggests that, while the act of poetry remains free, "the worth of the booty it brings back from the inarticulate will depend upon the emotional capacity, intellectual resource and general civilisation maintained between the raids".

Ana has a further reason which she offers: "Students respond to the culture they are part of and they have to understand it intellectually. If they don't get to the root of it they will think they are discovering the black powder – when the Chinese invented it hundreds of years ago."

There are also parallels between her work as an artist and her work as a teacher, or perhaps they are the same thing: "Experience cannot be transferred – you can share it. That is the whole thing about bad teaching – they think they can transfer experience, and here there is an implication of power because there is an attempt to dominate. And yet the idea that you can simply find the means yourself to flourish, based on gifts or talent, is one I find very doubtful. There is a paradox. Talent is not enough. Creative art is a work of the mind. The idea that here is so strong, that there is a division between being academic and being artistic, I find very difficult to understand. Also I find the terminology very dubious. It would be better to say a 'creative person', because anyone can be creative. I felt the need to establish a ground within which the mind is challenged. You should always be in unknown territory, otherwise you develop habits, and habit makes the mind grow stiff. We want in an art school *continuous challenge*. The idea is to create an environment where students and all of us feel capable and confident enough to explore. If we are successful we will have people who are independent in their thought. I think that is the most sophisticated way of education. You are going to form a society where people can make judgements through sensitivity. A trained mind, scholarship, implies sensitivity."

The Banquet, study for sculpture, 1982

Students were therefore encouraged to reflect, research, consider social, historical, philosophical, literary and related issues as much as the aesthetic or tactile properties of the work. Ana always suggested that the 'work' is not simply the object produced in the studio, that by this time the 'work' has already been done in the spiritual and intellectual efforts surrounding the visible activity. Students received a mixture of the most English of cultural environments, of landscape and life-room, permeated by the most 'foreign' philosophy and practice, the opposing polarities of a powerful field, which reflect the experience of Ana's own education.

In her professional life as a teacher Ana is punctual, when she can remember where she is supposed to be, intellectual, inspiring and rigorously truthful, pushing half-truths away with critical ferocity. The life-room at Norwich School of Art became a place for research and rediscovery of the figure as metaphor and imaginative expression, with its roots in thought, ritual and magic. The School has plaster casts of the Elgin Marbles, the whitened receptacles of an English tradition, and also the routes to European and classical histories of the mythological, sensual and intellectual.

We thought that some of the best and most interesting of English art is to be found in medieval buildings, in the narrative sculpture of roof bosses, in doorways, corbels and windows, the religious, pagan and secular imagery, the mixture of epic and everyday life, the green men, the squabbling husbands and wives, the smiling portraits that look out from the arches of Norfolk churches. Here was sculpture of coloured painted stone not at the periphery of a tradition as some would propose, but at its heart. We liked its grace and humour.

The Banquet, 1985, detail

Looking at Ana's work, *The Banquet, Every Man Wears a Head on His Shoulder*, many are struck by their darkness. Some find the mixture of power, sexuality, impure technique, distasteful or disturbing. Why such grotesque subjects? Why so dark? Why so many teeth? Dr Helen Boorman has referred to 'the little murders'. Just as in English art there is to be found a tradition of coloured figurative sculpture, narrative sculpture, so there is to be found a tradition of big and little murders. At the heart of the Christian religion is a murder and betrayal, and the churches and cathedrals are inscribed with the stories of little betrayals which are also part of the fabric of modern life. Glances, gestures, sentences, written or spoken, the hidden narratives are the stuff of which her work is made; observations of how each can be victim and torturer. However discreet English life can be, it cannot conceal its practices entirely. Hogarth or Blake knew as many of them. On Ana's bookshelves, between Foucault and Bertrand Russell, is a collection of Edward Lear's observations:

> There was an old man of Whitehaven
> Who danced a quadrille with a raven,
> But they said it's absurd
> To encourage the bird
> So they smashed that old man of Whitehaven.

Some exercise of power.

The Banquet, 1985, detail

Ana's figures represent, I think, an essentially transcendental view of human beings as mixtures of shifting good and evil. Throughout the whole oeuvre there is a strain of humour and of optimism that comes from facing the worst there is to see. In the most recent work, *Man and His Sheep* and the lovely series of painted boxes, grace and gentleness emerge as primary sources of the work. As Sarah Webb has written, "We are told of death in the title, yet here we see life renewed".

The absurd is never very far away. The teeth for the sculptures come from dentists' suppliers, trays of them in different colourations and states of wear. Hilarious at tea in the studio. A garage mechanic once strayed in, repaired the hoist and stayed to enjoy the horror. A letter from a former neighbour says, "I hope you aren't still making your monsters". Often in the responses of 'ordinary people' there is a sense of delight which comes from the recognition of experience.

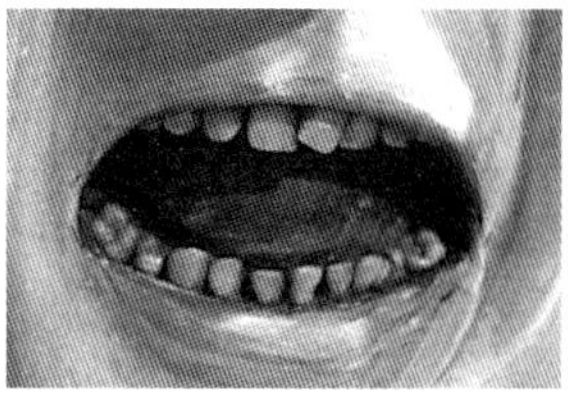

Detail of teeth

The stereotyping of artists and writers always carries a danger. Whilst Ana has her roots in Brazil, in her childhood and family, in Catholicism, in the fears and celebrations of another continent, the work is diminished if it is crudely categorised in this way. The work represents as much the divisions of Brazilian culture as its coherence. She speaks of the disparity between her education, which was French in structure, and the flat wilderness of the surrounding landscape, the Cerrado, in which she lived and which was the early source of her work.

"The system is rooted in Europe, it has not evolved from Brazil but from somewhere else, though it may have taken the accent of Brazil. Then when you leave the building you go out to confront this landscape and ecology that has nothing to do with what you have learned. The Cerrado isn't a jungle. It is in contrast to the European landscape which has been domesticated. Near Goiás everything is thin, uncertain, distorted, scared and fearful like an animal hunted. So we went from the school and confronted that. It makes you have a schizophrenic perception of things. There might be an attempt in my work to balance these things. Two things are juggling. One is the raw, that landscape and everything that is implied. You live with it and are part of it. The other side is the European thing you learn about, the intellectual pleasures of literature. Balance is the wrong word. There is an attempt to live with both, because you can't live in either one. You have to try to live with both extremes. You have lost the right to choose because you have been exposed to both."

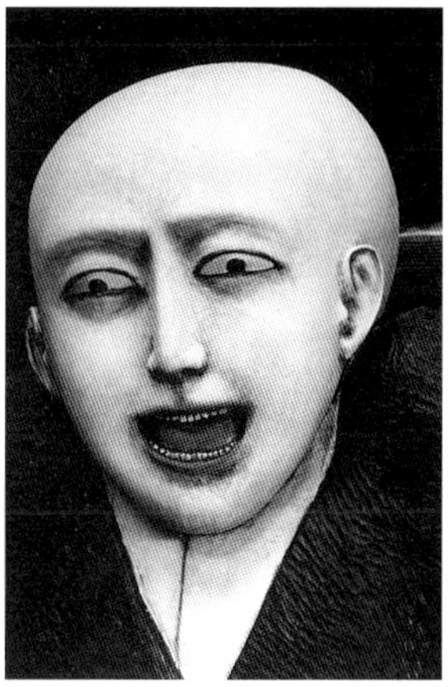

The Banquet, 1985, detail

There is a temptation to speak of magic realism as though it belongs to South America, to Lorca, Borges or Márquez, but this may be because traditions of realism within Western art and literature have become devoid of magic and therefore unrealistic. Ana's work belongs, through her education and experience, as much to Dante as to Márquez, as much to the meeting with the wandering souls of the first circle, as to the families of *One Hundred Years of Solitude*. Life is perceived to be a matter of some solemnity, within which each action or gesture carries its consequences, revelations and echoes. The drawing of a figure, the environment of a life-room, belong therefore to the imagination and to ethics as well as to the measurement of proportion or the acquiring of a skill.

"If you want to do anything in the physical world you have to master yourself. You have to go down that road and forget it. There is a paradox. Technique is the only thing you can teach. This is a very interesting point. I have not come to a conclusion. You can teach how to put a ground on a plate to make a cast or stretch paper or whatever. The thing is you can't do that out of context, which is the context of the vision of the person who is doing it. There this gets really difficult. If one looks very carefully at academies, one can see that there is a strategy, which to me is very materialistic – but the thing is, it doesn't work. After you have learnt your technique, what do you do with it? This is a curious thing. The other side of your mind pays a heavy price. You can kill the imagination in this way. It happens a lot in instrument playing, more so because it is so difficult to produce an acceptable sound. People spend a huge amount of time to do that. Then when it comes to the moment of freeing yourself of all that to make music, you can't do it, because you have lost your way already. You are, let's say, so conditioned to a particular way of doing things that

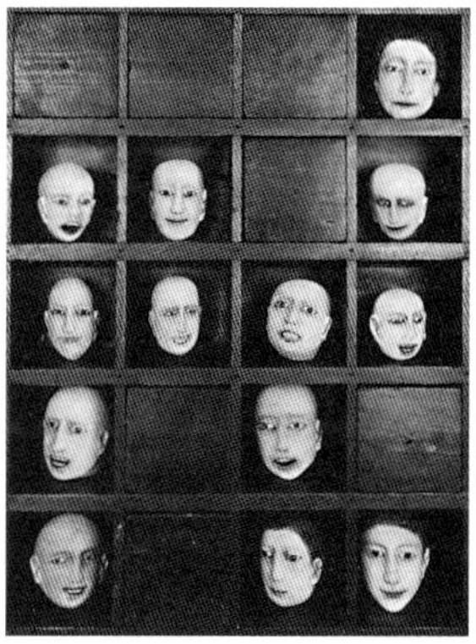

Box of Heads, 1983

the actual way of making music has lost its meaning. García Lorca says: 'The Duende' – the spirit – is not there'."

The work combines traditions of theatre, music, poetry and the visual arts in images of gentleness and ferocity within the structures of relationships of power. Leader and victim are sometimes interchangeable within the individual and group psychology. The relationship between *The Banquet*, which is primarily black and white and terrifying in its oppressive clarity, and the more recent *Man and His Sheep*, which is colourful and more overtly positive, may be seen as both spiritual and aesthetic development. Much of current Western culture seems either designed to conceal horror or to present it as aberrant human behaviour somehow separate from 'ordinary life'. Ana's work accepts horror as being within an ordinary and ancient framework, a tangible part of the everyday. Primo Levi in *The Drowned and the Saved* makes a direct and applicable parallel between the trusts maintained and betrayed in the concentration camps, and those to be observed in everyday life.

If the work is conceived of as theatre, the relationship between the actors, the individual pieces of sculpture must be examined. The work is much to do with 'sedimentation', of marks, of labour, of change of material, of surface, of colours. The surfaces of the heads are laid and overlaid with colours, each colour glowing through the ones above as in the Venetian style of painting. Pieces are made slowly, with respect to the craft of making, so that there is nothing superficial, and through this process of sedimentation something else occurs; figures transfer from work to work to appear in new guises. They mirror each other from group to group, like actors in a different act or drama. Across the roof of Norwich Cathedral the bosses are divided into fourteen bays, seven for the Old Testament, seven for the New, which reflect each other in subject matter. In each bay there is a central image surrounded by a circular narrative represented by the groupings of the bosses, and each individual boss, planned to be viewed from below, tells its story in a circular fashion. Behind the table are Herod and Herodias with the devils; before it are watchers and diners, and Salome, who appears twice, both dancing and carrying the head of John the Baptist.

The Banquet, study for sculpture, 1983 ▾

The bloated and constrained grotesques of *Every Man Wears a Head on His Shoulder* find themselves remade as the fat, overblown figures in *The Banquet.* The pontificating male in *The Longest Journey* reappears in *A Little Spell in Six Lessons* looking crestfallen and shamefaced as he receives instruction. The shepherd-god in the drypoint *Man and His Sheep* emerges unmasked but helmeted, shocked at the revelation of his role. The roles alter, the faces remain the same. Thomas Hardy says that the story of a face would make a fine poem of the passage of time. Borges, writing of the *Inferno*, describes how Dante has discovered that most of us are defined by an instant of our lives.

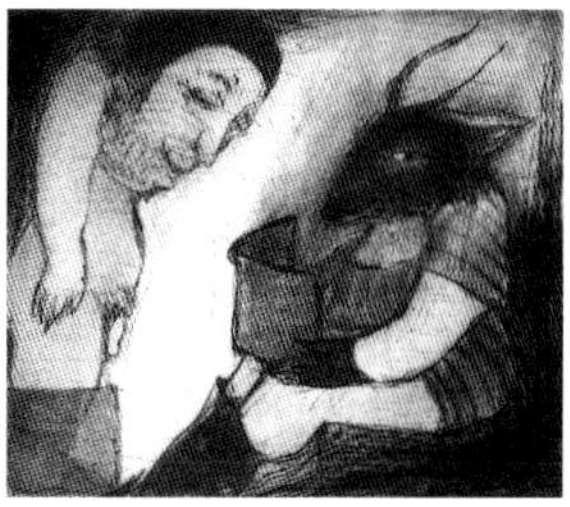

A Little Spell in Six Lessons 4, 1988

The most lasting quality of the sculptures as they lay on the studio floor, or began to stand in groups, was their appearance of vulnerability, despite the narrative of power in which they are engaged; and I felt that Ana had discharged her responsibility as a maker of art, just as she discharged her responsibility as a teacher. To quote her:

"That comes to the point perhaps – I was going to circumnavigate – the artist is going to attempt to demonstrate how dependable we are. When we look to a Fra-Angelico, or to a Picasso, or to a Goya, one senses the genuine work of art should convey the incredible paradox of being human, the frailty, the inner strength. It is a continuous testimony of humanity that we need that – all the time – to keep alive. That is a big responsibility. I was afraid to become pompous. You see it is through the work that dependability is conveyed. One of the things that is so terrifying about Fascism, the whole awful thing about Fascism, is this total absurdity, this pretence that we are invulnerable, and I think that what I find so marvellous about art is that it shows how vulnerable we are. If there is a responsibility it is more at that level."

Every Man Wears a Head on His Shoulder II, 1981

References:

Seamus Heaney: *The Government of the Tongue*, Faber and Faber, 1988, p.170.

Primo Levi: *The Drowned and the Saved*, Michael Joseph, 1988.

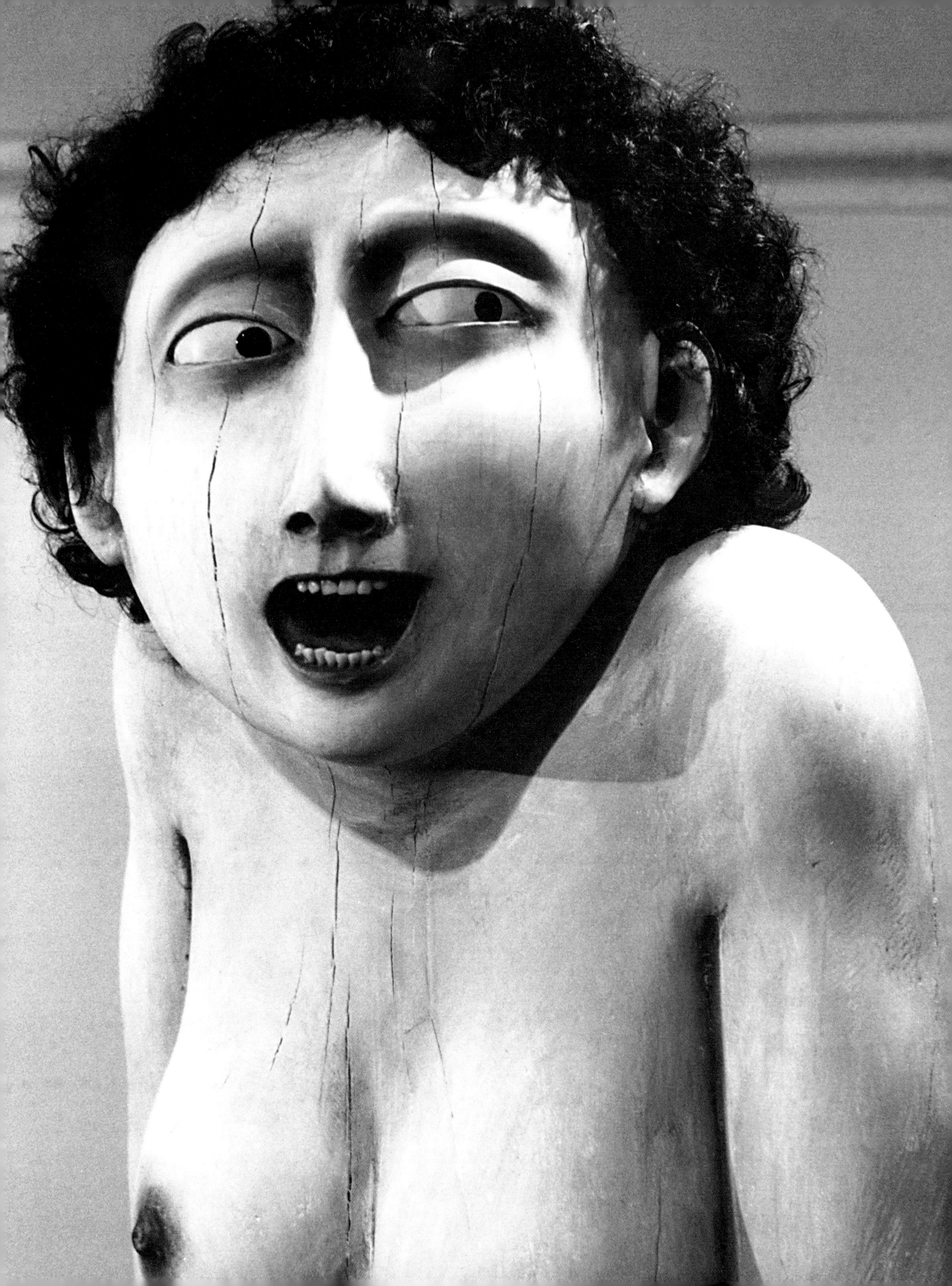

Ana Maria Pacheco

Chris Mullen

Firstly, some certain things. Ana Maria Pacheco came to Britain from Brazil in 1973. Since 1980 she has been producing groups of figures in carved and painted wood. The drawings and prints shown here primarily function as preparatory studies for those groups. *Some Exercise of Power* (not exhibited) was the first of these pieces to be selected for an exhibition of national significance, *Women's Images of Men*, ICA, London, 1980. She has taught at the Croydon School of Art and has been artist in residence at Trinity School, Leamington Spa. In May 1985 she was appointed Head of the Fine Art Department at the Norwich School of Art.

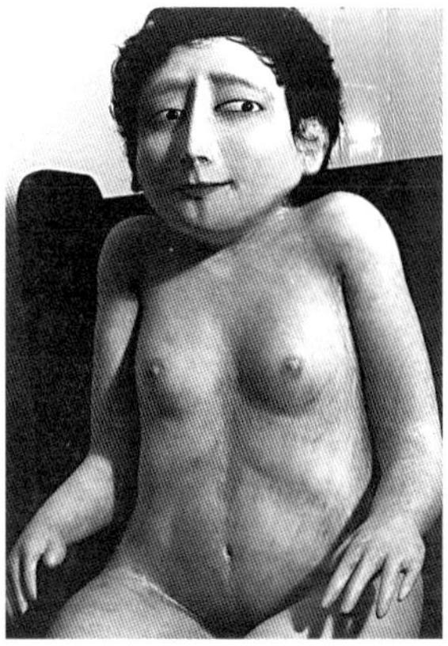

The Three Graces, Figure I, 1983, detail

Now, the ambiguities. In their form, grouping and expression, Pacheco's figures have been subjected to disturbing, even harrowing pressures. Political pressures culminate in the trial, sacrifice and devouring of the individual, helpless at the whim of the oppressor, the judge, the torturer. This arbiter of the fate of the individual may be provided in the sly tormentors of *Some Exercise of Power*, or may be transferred to you, the spectator. Psychological pressures between the figures intensify their confrontations. Above all, a leaden, gravitational pressure is applied, bearing down on victim and conspirator alike, on the rapt and on the terrified, the mute and the silenced.

This gravity, in both its senses, flattens, distorts and locates. Pacheco figures seem to take the strain on the head, the arms tense, without the mitigating gracefulness of the neck. The proportions, confusingly, are more those of the child than the adult, making more poignant the suffering, the drowning of innocence. This heavy force that acts upon them precludes action and absorbs noise; a permanent drawing in of breath rather than expulsion. In a more nourishing atmosphere, there would be hope of catharsis, resolution or a ritual cleansing.

Acrobats, 1983, detail

The ambiguities can be weighed in *The Three Graces* project, three figures to describe the female condition through the three ages of woman, seen in three basic states of inaction, sitting, lying and standing up. The women are located anywhere on the axis from Eve to Lilith, with perhaps a distant reference to the Annunciation. *Figure II*, lying transfixed on a mattress, serves as Saint and Sphinx, yet also is carnally on display.

The ambiguities of *Acrobats* balance on the spectacle of the paid performer in fancy pants, showbiz and politics. Denied the aerial grace of, say, Degas' *Miss Lola at the Cirque Fernande*, they take on the look of the sacrificial victim, or more particularly, the flayed forms of Mussolini and his mistress on the partisans' gibbet.

These ambiguities allow Pacheco's figures to skirt the excesses of melodrama and sentiment, most appropriate to our age, when evil issues from the mundane, the lounge suit and the balance sheet.

◂ *The Three Graces, Figure III,* 1983, detail

Ana Maria Pacheco

Vivien Lovell

It is ten years since Ana Maria Pacheco left Brazil. Since the last works she made there, several of them public commissions completed in the years 1967-73, her images have become increasingly more expressionistic, more radical. The ability to carve images on a monumental scale was evident, however, even from these first smoothly finished sculptures and reliefs depicting groups of women and children, organic and foetal in form. The acceptability of those early works can be contrasted with the unlikelihood of a public commission resulting from the present subject matter of her work. At a time when fashion in art is returning to figuration, Pacheco's work is still unfashionable. Since 1980 Ana Maria Pacheco has produced groups of figures in carved and painted wood; her large-scale charcoal and pastel drawings she regards as preparatory studies for the sculptures, although paintings have become more important of late. *Some Exercise of Power* is one of a series of works, which includes *Acrobats* and *The Banquet*, to reflect Pacheco's politics through her language of metaphor, and the first of her sculptures to be selected for an exhibition of national significance: *Women's Images of Men* (ICA 1980). A scenario of oppression and victimisation is presented in *Some Exercise of Power*: potent and unnerving as an image, it is typical of Pacheco's work in that its confrontational qualities demand a reaction on the part of the onlooker. The initial shock due to the scale and presence of these figures is superseded by an attempt to analyse their meaning, to decode the surface description of events. Presented with the irrational moment, the onlooker becomes part of the drama in the attempt to decipher the scene. The three figures relate to each other not simply through the roles ascribed to them (two menacing figures hover over their victim, bound and vulnerably naked at their feet); the similarity of treatment of the heads and facial features and the direction of the eyes from one to the other, shifting from conspiracy to tortured despair, describe the dependency of the relationship. These are disturbing, uncomfortable images. They ask questions of the onlooker rather than providing answers. Pacheco achieves her intention ultimately to disquiet, to "explore rather than confirm the expectations that onlookers bring with them".[1] She is insistent that the onlooker's interpretation is as valid as her own, that the fundamental ambivalence of meaning will find its own levels through the perception of others.

The assault on the viewer's sensibilities at first sight of the sculptures, modified subsequently to a gradual discovery and reflection, is comparable to Pacheco's own progress of working: the initial onslaught of axe upon wood, followed by discovery and shaping of form, paring down to finest detail, the setting of teeth and eyes, the painting of flesh, the sticking of hair. Distortion of form heightens the emotive power of the figures: enlargement of the head, disappearance of the neck, tension in the raised shoulders and shortening of the arms are all effected in *Some Exercise of Power*, *The Three Graces* and *Acrobats*. This reasoning of scale is also evident in the series of heads, the quiddity of each one achieved through scale as well as expressive elements and choice of materials.

Some Exercise of Power, study for sculpture, 1979-80

The inability of the onlooker to meet the gaze of any of Pacheco's figures increases their emotive strength; to be able to do so might admit objectivity or rationality of response. Obliqueness and opacity of glance imbue the figures with a universal, ancient and quasi-religious, quasi-pagan quality. Agate and onyx are sometimes used for the eyes in the later sculptures, adding to the air of precious, freshly-discovered

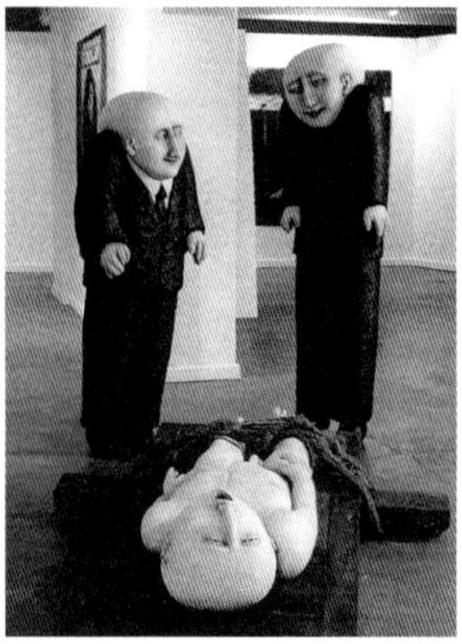

Some Exercise of Power, 1980, detail

mummified relic already inherent through the gessoed and painted wood with its cracks and fissures. Cultural references emerge in the work in a very fragmented way. Pacheco's vocabulary of images springs from a rich heritage: Baroque carved and painted effigies, Catholic, Protestant, pagan, Indian sources of imagery, influences from her upbringing in inland Brazil within a religiously 'mixed' family, are further enriched by childhood memories of masks and idols colouring pagan and religious festivals.

Traces of the artist's regard for the work of Goya and Francis Bacon are also perceptible but by no means dominant. Titles often underline Pacheco's use of irony: *Acrobats* comprises two inverted male figures, strung up by the feet to their 'trapeze' – a huge beam balanced between two trestles – the scaffold immobilising their act. Ridiculous details such as the finely-pointed boots and the red and white striped briefs appear to increase the *Acrobats* precariousness and vulnerability in the arena of conformity. Elsewhere in Pacheco's drawings and paintings the red and white striped motif appears as a handrail, hurdle or barre, as a means of dividing the space, emphasising the human role as that of performer or tamed animal. In the charcoal drawings of *The Three Graces* and in the second panel of the triptych *Untitled*, the female figures are further restricted by the imposition of what appear to be stocks

Some Exercise of Power, 1980, detail ▸

around their necks. These women/female archetypes appear to have been 'led on' or 'set up' in some way: at the same time they are seemingly in control of their situation, aware that they are acting out roles of chorus-girl conformity. Pacheco's use of the ancient theme of The Three Graces to describe the female condition through the three ages of woman is itself an ironic comment on the decorative, servile role of The Three Graces as depicted by male artists for centuries. Pacheco's use of irony and metaphor as expressionistic vocabulary obviates or short-circuits the need for a dialectical analysis of the work. In the same way that her work is instinctively feminist and political, in that it concerns itself with humanity rather than the particulars of a male-dominated or capitalist society, Pacheco herself does not affiliate to any political dogma or group. In a recent article about Ana Maria Pacheco and Judy Chicago, Rowena Serota wrote: "Her [Pacheco's] feminism is unequivocal – we are not educated into it by a laborious acquisition of data but propelled catastrophically into a new consciousness . . . Pacheco expresses both that which is most personal to her and universal for us. She achieves this because she does not try to teach us anything – the image operates on a primal level beneath the channels of language."[2] This primal level of communication operates powerfully through the sculptures but originates in the large charcoal drawings which exemplify Pacheco's energetic, hectic almost scribbled form of mark-making.

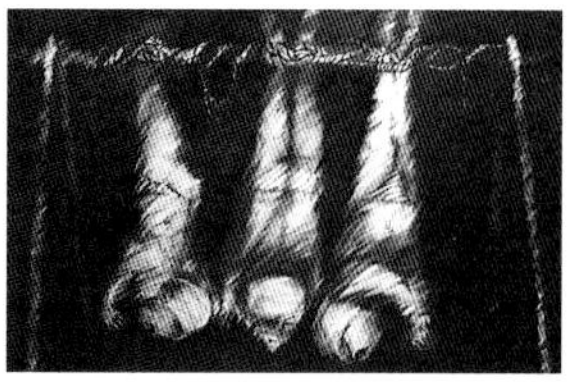

Acrobats, study for sculpture, 1983

The Three Graces, 1983

Left-to-right downward-sloping marks characterise these works, defining forms which emerge through chiaroscuro and hover, dramatically lit, on the edge of the picture plane. The charcoal marked figures convey even greater ambiguity than the sculptures, portraying "the divide between drama and melodrama . . . the mis-match of realities, of expectations in everyday life."[1]

Pacheco's strength in her "total integrity of feeling and action mediated through her charcoal lines"[2] carries through the momentum from the sketches to the painting of *The Banquet,* a superb evocation of the boardroom mentality of bureaucracy, emblematic of power structures, the four figures pawing over a supine form on the table. The inscription 'Eat, eat the flesh of Kings . . .'[3] sharpens the analogy to the Last Supper and to the image of a society feeding off itself. Pacheco has brought us to the extreme, marginal standpoint from which she operates as an artist and an outsider. These works, and the sculpture installation of *The Banquet* which has still to be made, promise to be Pacheco's most political, compelling and disturbing work to date.

Notes

1 Ana Maria Pacheco, catalogue statement: *Women's Images of Men,* ICA, London, 1980.
2 Rowena Serota, 'Feminism in Women's Art – A Question of Having or Being', 1983.
3 Revelation, Ch.19, v.17-18.

Acknowledgements

Kathleen ADLER

Head of Education at the National Gallery, London. She has written extensively on many aspects of French Impressionism including *Pissarro in London* (National Gallery, 2003) and *Impressionism* (National Gallery, 1999). Other publications include *Manet* (1986), *Berthe Morisot* (with Tamar Garb) (1987) and *Unknown Impressionists* (1988). She is currently working on a major exhibition on American painters in Paris, which opens in 2006.

'Ana Maria Pacheco: Dark Night of the Soul', in *Dark Night of the Soul*, Salander-O'Reilly Galleries, New York, 2003.

Helen BOORMAN

MA Material Culture Course Leader and Principal Lecturer in Critical Studies at Norwich School of Art and Design, Norfolk.

'Unfolding the Magic Spell: Imagery and Imagination in the work of Ana Maria Pacheco' in *Sculpture, Paintings, Drawings & Prints 1980-1989,* Pratt Contemporary Art, 1989, pp 7-11.

Andrew BRIGHTON

Andrew Brighton has been writing about art since the 1970s. He has written books on Francis Bacon and Picasso and has published articles and reviews in *Art in America, Studio International, New Art Examiner, London Review of Books, Art Monthly* and the *Guardian.* He is a contributing editor for *Critical Quarterly*. He has taught both art history and practice in various universities. In 1994 he joined the Tate. In 2003 he left his position as Senior Curator: Public Events at Tate Modern to write full-time.

'The Work of Ana Maria Pacheco', in *Work by Ana Maria Pacheco, Text by Andrew Brighton,* Pratt Contemporary Art, 1994.

Frances CAREY

Head of National Programmes at the British Museum; formerly Deputy Keeper of Prints and Drawings with responsibility for the Modern Collection.

'Introduction': *Sculpture, Paintings, Drawings and Prints 1980-1989,* Pratt Contemporary Art, 1989, pp 5-6.

John CLARK, FAHA, CIHA

Professor in Art History and Theory at the University of Sydney, where he teaches Asian Art History.

'For Ana, my sister, my friend', 2000. *Postwest,* no.19, 56-61, 2001.

David ELLIOTT

Director of the Mori Art Museum, Tokyo, Japan. He was Director of The Museum of Modern Art in Oxford, England (1976-96) and Director of Moderna Museet [National Museum of Modern and Contemporary Art], Stockholm, Sweden (1996-2001). He has worked as an exhibition organiser, teacher, lecturer, broadcaster, editor and writer on art and culture. He has also been President of CIMAM (International Committee for Museums and Collections of Modern Art, International Council of Museums (ICOM)) since 1998.

'The Smile on the Face of the Tiger', in *In Illo Tempore,* Pratt Contemporary Art, 1994, pp 4-5.

Jane FARRINGTON

Art Curator and writer on art; formerly Principal Curator of Art at Birmingham Museum and Art Gallery.

'The Longest Journey', Pratt Contemporary Art, 1994. Published to accompany the exhibition at the Gas Hall, Birmingham Museum and Art, Gallery, 1994.

John GLEDSON

Translator and retired Professor of Brazilian Studies at Liverpool University.

Translated: 'Ana Maria Pacheco's 'Memória Roubada': A Latin American Work', (José Lobo, 2001) and 'Flowing to the Unknown: Streams of Change, Rivers of Communion' (Nicolau Sevcenko, 2001).

Paul HILLS

Professor of Renaissance art history at the Courtauld Institute, London. He has been Visiting Professor at the Institute of Fine Arts, New York, the Harvard Center for Renaissance Studies, Villa I Tatti, Florence and the Royal College of Art, London. He was formerly Senior Lecturer at the University of Warwick.

'Ana Maria Pacheco: Land of No Return', in *Land of No Return*, Salander-O'Reilly Galleries, New York, 2003.

'In Illo Tempore: ten paintings by Ana Maria Pacheco', in *In Illo Tempore*, Pratt Contemporary Art, 1994, pp7-11.

Amanda HOPKINSON

Director of the British Centre for Literary Translation at the University of East Anglia and the author of numerous literary translations and books on Latin American photography.

'Ana Maria Pacheco's Metamorphoses', Pratt Contemporary Art, 1998.

José LOBO

Poet.

'Ana Maria Pacheco's 'Memória Roubada': A Latin American Work', in *Memória Roubada*, State University of Goiás: Centre for Artistic Education, 2002.

Vivien LOVELL

Director of Modus Operandi, an independent arts consultancy providing artistic direction and a commissioning service to a broad range of clients.

'Ana Maria Pacheco' in *Ana Maria Pacheco* [Pratt Contemporary Art], 1983.

John McEWEN

Author and art critic. His books include monographs of Paula Rego and Michael Sandle.

Introduction: *Ana Maria Pacheco: Collected Essays*, Pratt Contemporary Art, 2004.

Chris MULLEN

Supervises studio based PhD research projects at the University of Brighton.

Introduction: *Ana Maria Pacheco*, Ashley Gallery, Epsom in association with [Pratt Contemporary Art], 1985.

Brendan PRENDEVILLE

Author of 'Realism in 20th Century Painting' and teaches in the Visual Cultures Unit at Goldsmiths' College, London.

'In the Region of Shadows', in exhibition catalogue, Pratt Contemporary Art, 2004.

Vivian SCHELLING

Cultural historian and lecturer in Third World Studies at the University of East London.

'Ana Maria Pacheco – in context', in *Twenty Years of Printmaking*, Pratt Contemporary Art, 1994, pp. 5-9.

Nicolau SEVCENKO

Historian and Professor at the Department of History at the University of São Paulo, Brazil, where he teaches Contemporary Cultural History.

Flowing to the Unknown: Streams of Change, Rivers of Communion, 2001. First publication.

Ian STARSMORE

Poet, author and artist. Lecturer for the Open University, Cambridge.

'Ana Maria Pacheco 'Inventing the Black Powder' – Art and Education', in *Sculpture, Paintings, Drawings & Prints 1980-1989*, Pratt Contemporary Art, 1989, pp, 13-17.

Cover text, 1991.

Dom Antony SUTCH

Parish Priest of Beccles, Suffolk. Benedictine Monk of Downside Abbey; formerly Headmaster of Downside School, Bath.

'Quietus est', Artist's Book, Pratt Contemporary Art, 2000.

George SZIRTES

Poet, critic and translator. He has written forty poems for the Artist's Book *A Modern Bestiary* (Pratt Contemporary Art, 2004). His most recent books of poetry are *The Budapest File* (Bloodaxe, 2000) and *An English Apocalypse* (Bloodaxe, 2002). Bloodaxe will also publish *Reel* in November 2004. His various awards include the Faber Prize for poetry and the European Poetry Translation Prize.

'Ana Maria Pacheco's The Longest Journey', in *The Longest Journey*, Pratt Contemporary Art, 1996.

Annela TWITCHIN

Art historian and lecturer.

'New and Recent Prints', extract published in exhibition catalogue, Pratt Contemporary Art, 2004; first publication in full.

Simon WILLMOTH

Director of Graduate Studies and Research at Norwich School of Art and Design.

'Circumnavigation: the poetics of exploration in the work of Ana Maria Pacheco', in *Twenty Years of Printmaking*, Pratt Contemporary Art, 1994.

Colin WIGGINS

Deputy Head of Education at the National Gallery, London.

'Reclaiming the Baroque: a drama in wood', (2001); first publication.

'Transformations', exhibition catalogue, Pratt Contemporary Art, 1998.

Selected bibliography

George Szirtes: *Exercise of Power: The Art of Ana Maria Pacheco*, Lund Humphries, 2001.

Nicolau Sevcenko: 'Trances, Traversals, Transports, Transgressions' in *Ana Maria Pacheco: Selected Works: Prints and Drawings*, (bi-lingual text); foreword by Heloisa Aleixo Lustosa, Museu Nacional de Belas Artes, Rio de Janeiro, Brazil, 2000.

David Elliott, 'Ana Maria Pacheco', catalogue text, Dak'Art Biennale 2000.

Ana Maria Pacheco in the National Gallery, National Gallery Publications, 1999; foreword by Neil MacGregor; essays: 'Terra Ignota: The Art of Ana Maria Pacheco' by Kathleen Adler; 'Working at the National Gallery', by Colin Wiggins.

George Szirtes, 'Human Nails', *Modern Painters*, Vol.12, No.3, Autumn 1999.

George Szirtes, 'Rites and melodies: The work of Ana Maria Pacheco', *Contemporary Art*, Vol.2, No4, 1994/5.

Richard Noyce, 'The Theatre of Ana Maria Pacheco', *Printmaking Today*, Vol.3. No.1, Spring 1994.

Peter de Francia, 'Some Exercise of Power', exhibition guide, Camden Arts Centre, London, 1991.

Linda Saunders, 'Ana Maria Pacheco', *Modern Painters*, Vol.3, No.1, Spring 1990.

Frances Carey, 'The Prints of Ana Maria Pacheco', *Print Quarterly*, Vol.V, 1988, 3.

Films

'Ana Maria Pacheco in the National Gallery', written and narrated by Colin Wiggins; 1999. Distributed by National Gallery Company Limited, London.

'Grace and Power: The Art of Ana Maria Pacheco': produced and directed by Clive Dunn, Seventh House Films, for Anglia Television, 1992-3.

'One Eye for the Devil and One for God': a documentary directed by Terry Bryan for Central Independent Television, 1984.

List of Works

Brief Biography

1943	Born in Goiânia, Goiás, Brazil.
1960-64	BA in Sculpture and Music.
1965	Postgraduate Course in Music and Education.
1966-73	Lecturer at the University of Goiás and the Federal University of Goiás, Brazil.
1973-75	British Council Scholarship to the Slade School of Fine Art, London.
1985-89	Head of Fine Art, Norwich School of Art, Norfolk.
1996	Appointed Fourth Associate Artist at the National Gallery, London (1997-2000).
1999	Honoured by the Brazilian Government with the prestigious Ordem de Rio Branco.
2000	Honorary Degree (Doctor of Letters), University of East Anglia.
2002	Honorary Degree (Doctor of Philosophy), Anglia Polytechnic University.
2003	Fellow, University College London.

Selected Solo Exhibitions

1983	Ikon Gallery, Birmingham
1985	Ashley Gallery, Epsom
1991	Camden Arts Centre, London.
	Museum of Modern Art, Oxford.
1992	Trondhjems Kunstforening, Trondheim, Norway.
1993	Oslo Kunstforening, Oslo, Norway.
1994	Norwich Castle Museum, Norfolk.
	The Gas Hall, Birmingham Museum and Art Gallery.
1994–96	*Twenty Years of Printmaking*, touring exhibition of prints.
1995	City of Plymouth Museum and Art Gallery.
1996	The Trout Gallery (Weiss Center for the Arts) Dickinson College, Carlisle, Pennsylvania, USA.
1999	Kilkenny Arts Festival, Ireland.
1999-01	National Gallery, London (touring).
2000	Museu Nacional de Belas Artes, Rio de Janeiro, Brazil
	Museu de Arte Contemporanea, Goiânia, Goiás, Brazil
2001	Ashmolean Museum, Oxford
	Blackburn Museum & Art Gallery.
2002	Salander-O'Reilly Galleries, New York, USA
2003	Salander-O'Reilly Galleries, New York, USA
2003–04	Oldham Art Gallery
2004	Brighton Museum & Art Gallery
2004	National Touring Exhibitions: *'Ana Maria Pacheco – Prints'* organised by the Hayward Gallery for Arts Council England; launched at Brighton Museum & Art Gallery

Selected Group Exhibitions

1980	Institute of Contemporary Arts, London, 'Women's Images of Men', touring.
1982	Hayward Annual, London.
1991-92	The British Museum, *Collecting the 20th Century.*
1995	Ormeau Baths Gallery, Belfast, Northern Ireland: inaugural exhibition.
1995-96	The British Museum, *Recent Acquisitions 1991-95.*

2000 Dak'Art 2000, (Dakar Biennale), Senegal, West Africa.
2001-02 *Absences*, Norway, touring group exhibition: sculpture.
2002 British Museum, *Queen of Sheba: Treasures from Ancient Yemen.*
2003-04 Kunsthalle Wien, *Sebastian: A Splendid Readiness for Death.*

Collections include

British Museum
British Council
Arts Council Collection
Government Art Collection
Tate Gallery
Victoria and Albert Museum
The Unilever Collection
South East Arts Collection
Ashmolean Museum, Oxford
Birmingham Museum & Art Gallery
Wolverhampton Art Gallery
Oldham Art Gallery
Castle Museum, Nottingham
New Hall Women's Art Collection, University of Cambridge
Norwich Castle Museum
Hat Hill Sculpture Foundation, Chichester
Harris Museum & Art Gallery, Preston
Whitworth Art Gallery, Manchester
Blackburn Museum
Wakefield Art Gallery
Itaú Cultural, São Paulo, Brazil
Museu de Arte Contemporanea, Goiânia, Goiás, Brazil
Universidade de Goiás, Goiânia, Brazil.
Universidade Federal de Goiás, Goiânia, Brazil
Municipal Museum, Goiânia, Brazil.
New York Public Library, USA
Fogg Museum at Harvard University, Cambridge, Massachusetts, USA
Cincinnati Art Museum, Ohio, USA
Sweet Briar College, Virginia, USA
The Vivian and Gordon Gilkey Center for Graphic Arts, Portland Art Museum, Oregon, USA
Setagaya Art Museum, Tokyo, Japan
Herzog Anton Ulrich-Museum, Braunschweig, Germany
Museum of Contemporary Art, Fredrikstad, Norway
Trondhjems Kunstforening, Trondheim, Norway.

www.prattcontemporaryart.co.uk
www.anamariapacheco.co.uk